ProMigraine
end migraine fast

Niamh Flynn

Disclaimer. The advice in this book is for educational purposes only. Always seek professional medical advice for the treatment of migraines. It is imperative to rule out all secondary pathologies and establish an official diagnosis of migraine prior to treatment. Once you have a diagnosis of migraine, it is advisable to continue working with your health care professionals to ensure the best care for you. Novel treatments and medications need to be considered carefully and it is advisable to seek medical guidance on the treatment plan you decide to pursue. Each individual is unique and at different stages of our lives we each have different requirements. Some treatments, such as beta-blockers for example may be contraindicated during pregnancy while magnesium is generally considered safe to take during pregnancy[36]. Combinations of treatments and medications also need to be considered carefully, for example, if magnesium is combined with metoclopramide it can worsen the migraines rather than improve them[36].

For Darragh

whose joie de vivre is a lesson in living

Foreword

by **Dr. Andreas Jahnke**,
Neurologist

Migraines are probably the most common headaches and their severity can vary between very mild pain and very severe symptoms that even may lead to attendance in the A/E of a hospital. Migraines are a huge negative economic factor as they can lead to sick-leaves lasting days. Therefore optimized treatment is necessary at earliest stage.

Migraines also show colourful symptoms not only including the headaches themselves but also including nausea, phono- and photophobia and even sometimes vertigo, paraesthesia, visual auras with zig-zag-lines and vision loss and in rare cases paralysis and speech disturbances.

As the usual approach of acute and prophylactic treatment of migraines is to use medications of different types there are also non-pharmaceutical treatments available which usually have no side effects and are not so expensive. They are good alternatives and can be also added to the pharmaceutical treatment.

They are not so well known in the public and this needs to be changed as especially psychotherapies including hypnotherapy are well established for chronic pain treatment.

Niamh's great merit is therefore to be involved in actual studies to measure the benefits of hypnotherapy on migraines and now to present a book summarizing the details of hypnotherapy in the treatment of migraines and to provide an up-to-date workbook.

As I have no doubt about the prophylactic benefit of hypnotherapy in pain treatment with its potential to reduce medication expenses and possible side-effects I therefore wish this book the success it has deserved.

Acknowledgements

I am very grateful to everyone who provided the support which allowed me the freedom to pursue this project. Any errors in this book are solely my own responsibility.

Maya Pankowska, your painstaking reading of the first draft, your comments and guidance were much appreciated and insightful. Writing has been a long held passion and something which, for me, could never have been categorised as work. When at a crossroads in my career earlier this year, Pádraic Ó Máille made the suggestion to write this book. Thank you Pádraic for guiding me to choose the most gratifying turn at that juncture.

As Thomas Merton put it so eloquently, 'No Man Is an Island'. Particular thanks to neurologist, Dr. Andreas Jahnke. As a former patient I am very fortunate to have had the benefit of your wisdom, kindness and guidance. Your support and interest in your patients' welfare is an example of medicine at its best. Thank you to Gavin Byrne of Red River Studios for the photo-shoot that was so much fun and the choice of photographs to use with the bio. You have an immense talent that I continue to be in awe of. The emotional support and encouragement provided by friends cannot be quantified. It has been invaluable and it is indeed a great treasure. That list is long but you know who you are! My deepest gratitude to all of you.

My greatest debt is to my parents, John and Deirdre Flynn, and siblings, Sinéad, Cian and Darragh whose unwavering support and innate graciousness has always ensured there was a solid launch-pad from which to explore any opportunity that life might present. What a precious gift. Thank you, sincerely.

About the Author

Niamh Flynn has a Masters degree in Business Administration (MBA) from the Michael Smurfit Graduate School of Business, Dublin, a Masters degree in Sports Medicine from the University of Sheffield (MMEDSCI), a Bachelor of Arts Degree (BA) in Psychology from NUI, Galway and a Diploma in Hypnotherapy and Psychotherapy (DHP). She is currently pursuing a Ph.D in the area of hypnosis for migraine at the National University of Ireland, Galway. Niamh also has several certificates in health and fitness. Her company, Bodywatch Ltd. was established in 1997. She has worked as a freelance journalist with many newspapers and magazines for many years and she currently operates from The Galway Clinic, Doughiska, Galway. She is a certified instructor (CI) with the National Guild of Hypnotists and teaches the internationally recognised NGH Certified Hypnotherapy Training Course in both Galway and Dublin.

Contents

THE FACTS
Part I

Introduction

"From a certain point onward there is no longer any turning back.
That is the point which must be reached."

Franz Kafka

(i)   Why the ProMigraine Programme was developed

The impetus to write this book came about as a result of personal experience with migraines, subsequent research as part of a post graduate PhD programme and a nudge from my colleague and friend, the ever ebullient, inspirational motivational speaker, Pádraic Ó Máille. What follows, I hope, will encourage and enable others to find their own way to alleviate the pain of migraines from their lives.

Inertia. This may well be one of the most debilitating words in the English dictionary. If you have migraines or if you know someone who does, you will be familiar with the abrupt and instantly crushing effect which migraines can exert. They can appear to strike out of nowhere and for no particular reason. The fact that science has failed to find one definitive cause for migraines is not helpful either. The pursuit of potions, pills and promises of instant relief has become a past-time for many of those suffer with this medical enigma. Hope is imminent nevertheless. The ProMigraine Programme is about providing an insight into the world of migraines from which a personal solution can be considered and extracted. Some of you, as a result of the programme will experience less severe and less frequent migraines and others will find that your migraines end completely and permanently. A former medical doctor who currently practises Ayurvedic medicine patiently explained to me during a consultation that while western medicine is very good at diagnosing, it then follows a process of treating symptoms rather than focusing on restoring health as is the ethos of much eastern medicine. Medicines can and do provide a quick solution for many people. However, they can be costly, they can trigger side effects and they are often unilateral in their function. This book is directed towards those interested in a comprehensive overview of migraines and those who wish to consider the multiple facets leading to and pertaining to their migraines. This information can then be used to create a personal plan, the aim of which is to decrease the severity, frequency and disability associated with the painful condition that is migraine.

Therefore, this ProMigraine Programme intends to educate. It will explore the physiological changes which occur prior to and during a migraine. It will also provide an overview of the current medical and alternative options available. Throughout the book, some scientific studies have been quoted to validate particular points and to provide you with references in the event that you would like to pursue information in any area in more detail. A workbook has also been included to correspond with each chapter so that you have the opportunity to take action and build a programme to effectively manage your migraines and create the lifestyle you wish to have. It may be a good idea to complete your workbook as you go along. The purpose of this is to help you understand your personal situation with respect to migraines and to build a plan that is unique to you.

(ii)   My own migraine journey

I have not had a migraine for over seven years. Nonetheless, the sudden, inconvenient onset of blurred vision, feelings of nausea and whirling sensations prior to the acute, intense black pain are still embedded in my memory and serve as a reminder to me to stick to my migraine programme and keep them at bay. As a migraine sufferer you will be familiar with the impulsive nature of the intense, chronic headache which can strike at any time. I remember one incident a long time ago when I called in to the manager of the local store where I shop in order to apologise for abandoning a basket full of groceries a few days beforehand. Although he seemed completely unperturbed saying that this was a regular occurrence in the store it begged the question as to how many other owners of neglected shopping baskets had fled to a darkened room because of migraines. Given that the statistics from the International Association for the study of Pain (IASP) record that approximately 13-18% of women and 5-10% of men are affected by migraines, the specious and snappy decampment from social situations may, in many instances, have a more banal explanation than creative imaginations could have conjured up in the past. Thankfully, after researching the area and receiving great advice from doctors and complimentary practitioners I took action and adapted several areas of my life which involved a much appreciated increase in sleep, osteopathic treatment and considerably less stress. That was the journey which subsequently banished migraines from my life completely. The intensity and frequency of migraines varies from person to person. The aetiology is poorly understood although there are several theories as to the cause of this pesky and painful affliction. It is often a case of each person finding a personal solution to restore function and alleviate pain. Your journey might well take a different route to mine but it could also lead you to the same destination; a life where migraines are a thing of the past - or at least a less frequent and less oppressive visitor to your door.

(iii) Taking action

I am rarely happy doing something just because I am told to and I do not believe I am alone in holding that attitude. Most of us need a reason to take action. It is essential to define your goals and what you wish to achieve from a migraine intervention. Is it merely pain relief you are searching for? If it is, then perhaps analgesic medication may well be the most efficient form of management for you. If your aim is to be more confident when going on holidays that you will be able to enjoy your time off then your plan will be quite different. Be clear about what you want to achieve. Blindly following an avenue apropos to nothing can be a waste of valuable time.

Subsequently, this ProMigraine Programme is designed to go some way towards helping you to understand the triggers and the patterns of your migraines and to consider why your migraines are occurring. It also intends, in a relatively simple manner to explore the physiological factors underpinning migraines and to uncover some of the treatment options currently available. Armed with this information you can create your own personal management programme to help you achieve your clearly defined goals. Perhaps these goals will involve a decrease in the frequency and intensity of your migraines, an elimination of the intertia caused by immobilization and a restoration of a sense of control in your life. If migraines are currently making your life miserable it is your vision of the future which will have a significant influence on the plan you decide to create.

(iv)   Two Steps, One Goal

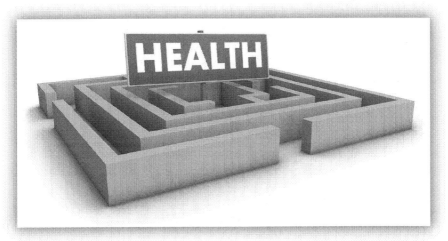

Consider the book as a road map of two stages. The first is about education and learning more about migraines. A voyage of discovery, if you like, to uncover how you got to where you are now given the frequency, duration and intensity of your migraines. The second part is about exploring and creating a map so that you can reach a place where you attain your ambitions be those fewer migraines or less severe migraines or both. In some instances, as several members of a focus group I worked with have found out to their amazement, migraines, when managed well, can disappear completely.

(v)   Monitoring Your Migraines

Many years ago, my affable accountant, at the end of his tether, reprimanded me rather suddenly during a routine meeting. With the deadpan expression of one who is weary at the end of the tax year, he asked me how I could expect to form any plan of action if I did not know where I was going and if I could not make up my mind about what I wanted. He was correct. His caring, albeit curt remark subsequently initiated a chain of events which changed my business for the better and opened up a delightful new world from there on in. That journey started with goal setting and a basic SWOT analysis. The plan to manage my migraines has followed a similar, successful path.

Despite the debilitating stymie which migraines can confer on their victim it is all too easy to move on quickly to routine daily demands once recovery ensues. The attempt to salvage all time left before the next one strikes and consumes more valuable hours and days is human. It is also inefficient. The definition of foolishness in the lay-mans lexicon is to expect a different result despite repeatedly performing the same ritual. Awareness and planning are integral to creating an effective ProMigraine Programme. Take your first step by locating a copy book to scribble on or use the workbook at the end of this book and track the frequency, duration and intensity of your migraines. It is also a good idea to look back retrospectively over the past month and from memory, recall how many hours and days were stolen from you by migraines. Then, make a list of all of the activities which were abandoned or neglected because you had to bury your head in the bed and seek solace in a dark room. Write everything down – even the demands you were delighted to relinquish... More about that later...

(vi)   Define your reason to end your migraines

It is time to get the diary or your workbook out again and answer a few questions. How badly do you want to eliminate migraines from your life? What benefits are there for you to free yourself from frequent pain? What benefits are there for you to hold on to the pain? Yes, you read the last question correctly. Pain is a warning sign and as such it is helpful.

What emerged from discussions with other migraine sufferers is that occasionally there is a benefit to having migraines. Indeed, migraines are draining, and yes, they may prevent you from doing the things you want to do. Absolutely, they are inconvenient and horrifically painful. However, they can also provide a very legitimate excuse to abandon unpleasant or routine jobs and impositions when one is completely overwhelmed. The truth hurts. The truth is also a great leveller. It can potentially provide a platform from which to generate the impetus for change and the development of a more efficient means of dealing with the demands of daily living – without pain. Life is busy; too busy at times. Scrambling along on the familiar Ferris wheel can seem somewhat tolerable in comparison to the potential mental and physical overload implicated by a change of direction. Ironically, the purpose of the original Ferris wheel is far removed from our current interpretation of a fast paced hamster wheel with an occluded view. The Ferris wheel was designed by Chicago based civil engineer, George Washington Gale Ferris, Jr. in the late 19th Century as a slow moving observation construct with an expansive view of the world. The pace of the original Ferris Wheel may well be the pace to aspire to when it comes to treading the various elements of our migraine-free lifestyle.

(vii)   Design a life without migraines

When it comes to migraines we have a choice. We can continue as we are; content with familiarity and its associated trade-off to tolerate pain or we can slow down and disembark. It is about instant versus delayed gratification. Disembarkation affords the time to identify and disengage from the factors contributing to the pain and allows the freedom to choose a different vista and create a new plan of action to manage migraines.

One lady who suffers with migraines told me how she sometimes felt guilty that her eldest daughter had to babysit her siblings when migraines struck. At the same time this weary mother was honest enough to admit that it was a relief to get a break from the routine and chaos of minding the children because there was nothing she could do when a migraine surfaced except retire to bed, draw the curtains and stay there quietly until the searing pain had subsided. Her story is not an isolated one. Our subconscious mind is astonishingly adept at finding ways to restore balance.

What would life be like without migraines? The picture you are painting might be good or bad. For the lady mentioned in the previous paragraph it might mean less respite from day to day routine and increased stress of a different kind. Or it may mean more freedom to make decisions regarding a change in career, more time to socialise or more time to simply relax. It is your plan. You are the architect and you can imagine and design the type of life without migraines as you choose.

(viii) Knowledge is power

There is often a tendency to fear the things which we don't understand. Fear can lead to anxiety and stress, and stress is one of the main triggers for migraine. The solution? Awareness and education. Awareness lessens fear. Reduced fear, in turn, facilitates learning and learning leads to progress. Have you ever found yourself retracting from circumstances or reacting defensively to a situation simply because you felt at a disadvantage due to a perceived lack of knowledge? Yes, by all accounts we need shortcuts in order to survive. The tried and tested heuristics can shorten our journeys. When those journeys do not bring us to where we want to be however, it is time to look outside the mainstream and to make it personal. Do you really want to visit the same destination that everyone else visits time and time again and experience the exact same situation that the masses have decreed as acceptable? When those situations involve a trade-off of discomfort in lieu of time saving exercises in the short-term, perhaps that is the way to go. Indeed that is the solution provided by medicine. Unpleasant side effects are tolerable because they are the lesser of two evils at a moment in time. The less travelled road might be bumpy, time consuming and arduous initially but it is deeply personal, and ultimately you are in control of choosing the destination and deciding how far you are willing to travel in order to get there. By educating yourself as much as possible it is possible for you to make an informed decision about the trade off between an initial time investment to discover the reasons for your own migraines and the best path for you in order to manage them with or without medication.

In his seminal book 'The Biology of Belief', author Bruce Lipton, a former medical professor, explores the impact which our environment and our thoughts exert on our bodies at the deepest cellular level. We can, he explains, change our physiology by changing our thinking. Mr. Lipton's ability to share his insights on quantum physics and cell biology in a simple way so that people without a background in science can understand it, is in itself, a lesson in how to teach. The author describes a pivotal moment of his graduate school education when he was learning to clone stem cells. His professor and mentor Irv Konigsberg explained to him that when the cultured cells being studied were ailing, that the first place to look for the cause was to the cells' environment, not to the cells themselves.

Both professor and student turned educator are correct. When the plant which needs a lot of sunlight and water is placed in a dark corner and is deprived of these essentials, it will wither and die. The same plant, placed in the environment which provides all it requires fundamentally, will both survive and thrive as a healthy plant. Lipton's philosophy holds that our DNA is influenced by the energy in the environment in which we base ourselves and in the case of human beings, that DNA is also influenced by the energy evoked through the thoughts which we think.

Michel Thomas, the prolific polyglot of the 20th century, understood the power of conditioning and the need to educate oneself in order to make informed decisions.

Christopher Robbins, Thomas's biographer recalls in 'Man of Courage' how, even from a young age, Michel was never interested in believing the first thing he was told. Nor indeed, was he a slave to mass ideology. Born to a headstrong and highly independent mother whom he adored, he was largely self-educated. Despite qualifying for a place in chemistry at University, he was not able to afford the fees and studied philology, philosophy, archaeology and the history of art instead. His thirst for knowledge was unquenchable. Only when he was satisfied that he had read sufficiently around any topic, would Michel then form his own opinion. His life story is one of immense courage. A survivor of concentration camps and intolerable torture, among other extreme experiences, Michel Thomas adamantly and consistently refused to compromise his beliefs. The fact that his belief systems were so solidly based in education and his willingness to explore things with an open mind can only have been supportive in his ability to maintain his dignity and integrity in the face of perpetual adversity.

(ix)   Work migraine balance

An atavistic work ethic is an admirable trait - when you are working. When you have to take time off work because of migraines, the ardent work rate is curtailed. If you were to add up all the hours you are out of action each month because of migraines what would it amount to? If you were to salvage those lost hours by managing your migraines effectively and adopt a less aggressive approach to work how much more effective could you be? You may have to forfeit the short-term gains of a well-intentioned antipathetic energetic work practice, but over a month imagine what you could achieve.

Sometimes as we alluded to earlier, migraines give the perfect opportunity to avoid certain situations. Denial can be like pressing 'replay' on the playlist option of your iPod – you can expect the same songs in the same sequence with one hit of a button. It is highly unlikely that any migraine patient would consciously desire or use the torment of migraines as a deliberate avoidance strategy. Nevertheless, the brain seeks balance and if certain situations are perceived as stressful, migraines can be a seemingly legitimate way of your body and brain telling you – and those around you - that enough is enough. When you are filling out your workbook be specific. If you can spot situations where a migraine is preferable to the alternate then maybe it is time to address rather than avoid the situation or experience. Once clarity is restored, your mind is in a better state to search for alternate solutions and ultimately restore balance.

The intention behind this ProMigraine Programme is to educate and inform so that you too can move forward fully armed in the pursuit of a life where you control or in some instances, perhaps completely eradicate your own migraines. Part of this education involves an insight into the current physiological paradigms of migraine. The inchoate information currently available is a mere stepping stone in the path to becoming an efficient manager of this pain. Nonetheless the information which is available can be a useful when designing a strategic plan.

What Is Migraine?

(i)   Migraine versus Headache

Diagnosis of migraine and headache is complex. In fact there are a multitude of categories and sub-categories which a neurologist or pain specialist will consult in order to diagnose your pain. If the pain in your head is severe and is accompanied by vomiting, nausea and dizziness this may be, but will not always be a sign of migraine. The most common type of headache is a tension-type headache and even this diagnosis can be subdivided into infrequent episodic tension-type headache, frequent episodic tension-type headache, chronic tension-type headache and probable tension-type headache. And that is only one division of the primary headaches. There are many more. You get the picture! What is worth realising is that, irrespective of whether a diagnosis is headache or migraine people will vary in the way in which they deal with the pain and a visit to your neurologist to put your mind at ease can be a very positive step. They will be able to assess you properly. Headaches and migraines are very treatable but there are sometimes differential diagnosis that can be missed with migraines like minor stroke, intracranial bleeding or subarachnoid haemorrhage and glaucoma (increased eye pressure). Once the latter have been ruled out and migraine is the established diagnosis the great news is that some changes in lifestyle can make a massive difference to the frequency and severity of migraines.

(ii)   Classic versus Common Migraine

The International Headache Society[62] notes that the diagnostic criteria of migraine include at least two attacks if with aura and five attacks if without aura, lasting between four and seventy two hours, with characteristics of pulsating quality, with moderate to severe intensity, aggravated by physical activity and associated with nausea. Once your neurologist or pain specialist has given you a diagnosis of migraine it is useful to note whether the migraine is a classic or common one. The common migraine is one which satisfies the criteria outlined by the International Headache Society, and which is generally unilateral and may or may not be accompanied by nausea. The classic migraine is the same as the common migraine but is accompanied by neurological features often referred to as an 'aura'. You will know from experience what an aura is if you have classic migraine. Aura describes the auditory, visual and sensory hallucinations which are characteristic of migraine. When we refer to auditory hallucination, for someone with a migraine who is in the aura stage an example would be the gentle cry of a baby suddenly becoming intolerable and grating. Visual hallucinations take the form of obscured sight so the individual might be able to see a part but not all of an object or an object might look temporarily distorted. Sensory hallucinations can include vertigo and indistinct, uncomfortable sensations in the hands, arms or indeed other parts of the body.

(iii)   Stages of migraine

You might experience one or all of the stages of migraine and once you recognise the stages your own plan becomes easier to formulate. Five stages have been identified.

Stage 1 Prodrome Stage.
Up to 60% of migraine sufferers have a prodrome but it is a frequently neglected stage when an inquiry is made into migraine history[54]. The Prodrome phase is about emotional symptoms. There may be changes in your mood and you may experience very high energy levels or very low energy levels. Food cravings can also be quite intense.

Stage 2 Aura Stage

The aura can take the form of auditory, sensory, tactile or visual hallucinations as outlined previously. If for example visual hallucinations are present you might see flashing lights or zigzag lines in front of you. This stage usually occurs about twenty to sixty minutes prior to the migraine.

Stage 3 Migraine

The migraine can last anywhere between four and seventy two hours. There is a throbbing pain and most people will quickly look for a quiet and dark room away from sunlight while the migraine is experienced.

Stage 4 Resolution Stage

The migraine can often stop after the individual has gotten sick or after sleep.

Stage 5 Postdrome Stage

Once the migraine has gone the recovery begins. Fatigue, difficulty concentrating and gastrointestinal symptoms are typical of this stage.

(iv)   Migraine Triggers

Now that you have a clear picture of migraine stages and symptoms, it will soon be time to look at your lifestyle and the parts of your life which may be triggering your migraines.

Following exhaustive consultations with migraine sufferers on an individual and on a group level, some of the triggers identified include but are not limited to:

- Nutrition
- Sleep
- Holidays /Travel
- Exercise
- Stress
- Injury to head and neck
- Medication
- Weather
- Physical Exertion

Once you identify those which are relevant to your own migraine pattern, other factors will determine your success with your migraine management programme including:

- Time management
- Environment
- Balance
- Choice management

We will explore these contributory factors throughout the book and as you read each chapter you should gain a greater insight into why each of these factors could be contributing to your migraines and the alternatives available to you as you build your personal migraine management plan.

Most people who suffer with migraines will have stories to share about other migraineurs they know who will have a migraine attack if they eat a certain food, do not get enough sleep or are stressed. These factors and many other factors are valid considerations for anyone wishing to take control of their migraines. If you are afflicted by migraines, take solace in the knowledge that the solecisms and anomalies buried in the anecdotes and research can now potentially be a source for consideration rather than confusion. One study[71] in India interviewed 182 migraine patients to gain an insight into the factors which trigger migraines. Their findings revealed that 160 of the 182 people they spoke with were aware of specific triggers for their migraines, and more than two triggers were present in 34.4% of the patients. Emotional stress was the most pervasive factor with 70% of respondents blaming it for their migraines. Fasting was found to be a contributory factor in 46% of patients. For 52.5% of patients, physical exhaustion or travelling were the culprits. 44.4%, blamed sleep deprivation, 12.8% linked their migraines with menstruation and 10.1% found that weather changes were responsible for migraine attacks.

(v)   Physiology of pain

To date, the pathway which pain takes is unknown. What is generally accepted is that pain is a multidimensional experience. What we experience emotionally and physically and how we think are intertwined.

It would seem logical therefore when considering an intervention programme addressing pain that the plan should incorporate emotional, physiological and cognitive dimensions.

As you can imagine, it would be possible to write several text books explaining the intricacies of the physiological and psychological pathways along which pain travels from onset to experience. Suffice it to say there are thousands of books out there which already satisfy the need for this body of knowledge very well and whose authors have studied the neuroscience, physiology

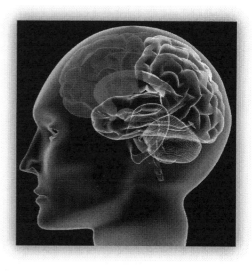

and anatomy of pain in greater detail. What I am describing here is a simplistic overview with the sole aim of providing a very basic understanding of how pain manifests. Subsequently, the mechanisms by which treatments such as acupuncture and hypnosis exert their effects should become clearer.

Migraines aside, when we sustain an injury, a certain threshold is crossed and nerve receptors will carry the information along fibres in the body known as A delta, A beta and C fibres. When the information reaches the dorsal horn in the spinal cord, the information is then passed on to the brain via the spino-thalamic tract. The thalamus in the brain is the initial port of call. It is a bit like a mail sorting office so when the information reaches this holding place, the office then points in towards the appropriate destination. Those destinations include brain structures known as the Insula, the Anterior Cingulate Cortex, the Pre-frontal Cortex and the Somatosensory Cortex.

Each of these destinations has a specific selling point, much like various cities around the world might be known for a particular characteristic. Think Las Vegas for entertainment, New York for shopping, Vancouver for scenic views and so on. Even though these cities are unique in their own way they are connected by transport systems and communication systems. So too with the brain. Various parts of the brain will interact with one another to create an experience that is unique to you. Once you understand how some of the areas of the brain work and how an increase or a decrease of activity in those areas will shape emotional and behavioural responses, this should help in understanding how complex an issue pain actually is and why a multidisciplinary approach to managing migraines can work extremely well.

Brain Parts and Pain

The Insula
The insula is a small part of the brain attributed with a variety of functions including activation of the pain matrix, interpretation and transformation of sensations into emotions e.g. a horrible taste might be interpreted as revulsion by the brain. In terms of pain, when the information reaches the insula, it appears to be responsible for interpreting how well someone feels that they can cope with the pain and fundamentally, what behaviours they believe they can and cannot do as a consequence of the pain. This relates to the feelings of disability that accompany any type of pain, including migraines. This is the part of the brain to blame if you decide that because of your migraine, you cannot do something that you would ordinarily be able to do.

The ACC
The anterior cingulate cortex (ACC) is central to problem solving. Scientists often discover how a part of the brain functions when that part of the brain is ablated or damaged. When the ACC is damaged or ablated, studies have shown that the affective (emotional) aspect of pain is compromised or ineffective. Most of us will have ACC regions of the brain which are fully intact and operational so information about pain delivered to the ACC will elicit emotions about pain, for example feeling disheartened, angry or sad.

Pre-frontal Cortex

The pre-frontal cortex has been highlighted as an area of the brain involved in selective attention. Some people have a great ability to focus in on one scene or object and to exclude or filter out all extraneous information about them even in the noisiest surroundings. Others become more easily distracted. The ability to selectively attend, like a zoom lens on a camera, is associated with this part of the brain. The degree to which one can or cannot focus intensely varies from person to person and indeed from situation to situation. In terms of pain, the prefrontal cortex assigns meaning to the pain so when the information is passed from the sorting house to the pre-frontal cortex, this part of the brain is responsible for initiating the thoughts the person might have about the pain and how it will affect what they can or cannot do. It is calculating the future repercussions of a behaviour or set of behaviours and assessing what you can or cannot do.

Somatosensory Cortices

This is the part of the brain which monitors the intensity of the pain. In a study[33] using PET scan imagery, researchers found that specific changes of activity were recorded in this area when suggestions about the intensity of the pain sensation were given in a state of hypnosis.

(vi) Physiology of migraines

Just as science has some way to go before we truly understand the complexity of how pain operates, the absolute cause of migraines is also a mystery. There are several theories nevertheless, and these can contribute to our understanding of what is happening when a migraine attack occurs.

When one member of a family presents with migraine, there is a good chance that other family members will have presented with a history of migraines at some point. Migraine has been linked to a complex genetic susceptibility[19]. However, if you do suffer with migraine, remember that environment plays a part also. A genetic pre-disposition to migraines does not guarantee that you will suffer with migraines. Even if you do suffer from migraine attacks it is not a life sentence. With careful analysis and good planning it is possible to create your own migraine programme to manage your migraines effectively.

There are vascular, neurological and serotonin based theories about why someone will suffer with migraine. A concept called cortical spreading depression (CSD) has also been implicated as a mechanism behind the aura aspect of migraine[6]. An incomplete but simplified explanation of cortical spreading depression is when the neurons in the cortex stop firing immediately after they have been firing rapidly. It is almost like they are taking a rest after completing a speed test.

The serotonin hypothesis for migraines holds that when there is a sudden imbalance in the serotonin levels of the brain, the blood vessels respond and pain ensues. For example, imagine that the serotonin levels rise as a result of stress. This increase in serotonin will cause blood vessels to contract and the pain threshold decreases. Serotonin can cause vasoconstriction and vasodilation of blood vessels. Before a migraine, serotonin levels have been shown to be very high and during a migraine the serotonin levels drop dramatically. Many of the drugs currently prescribed for migraines act to redress the imbalance of serotonin.

(vii)   Genetics and migraine

We know the triggers which can cause migraine but why are some people susceptible and others immune to specific triggers? Genetics and phenotype are the felons. Phenotype is the word used to describe how an organism appears due to the interaction of environment and genetics. Twin studies give us great insight into how the environment will affect the genotype we are born with. So while some of us may be *more likely* to experience migraine because of our genes, it does not necessarily mean we actually *will* experience migraine. The genome-wide association study (GWAS) often involves a control group so one group with a disease are compared with a similar group who do not have the disease. Despite the findings of a recent study[15] citing evidence for a weak association between migraine and 3 single nucleotide polymorphisms, another study[48] published one year later points out that a meta-analysis of six samples, also by GWAS, did not find evidence for genetic markers with migraine. The author of the latter study, Merikanges, also emphasises the fact that there are still major difficulties involved in understanding the underlying cause(s) of migraine. It is likely that a number of genes (polygenic) are responsible for contributing to migraine and currently the genes being investigated are those associated with neurotransmitter, vascular and hormonal function[58].

While the scientists pursue their curiosity about our genetic predisposition for migraine, the evidence for environmental influence on migraine expression is overwhelming and, while we can do little about the genes which we have been given, we can certainly influence our environment and the hold which these genes do or do not have over us. So, whether specific genetic markers are discovered or not, we can take comfort in knowing that if we suffer from migraine then we can, if we wish, muffle the genetic expression somewhat by observing and altering our lifestyle and our environment.

Economic Impact Of Migraine

"The poorest man would not part with health for money, but the richest would gladly part with all their money for health."

Charles Caleb Colton

Estimate the Economic Impact On Your Life

What are you losing financially because of the days lost to migraine? Given that the incidence of migraine is higher in lower socio-economic groups[66] and that in the US alone, migraine is believed to cost the economy $13 billion annually[65], having migraines is costly for the individual and for society at large. It is another chicken and egg situation. Does having migraine lead to loss of income because of missed working days and disability or does a low income lead to stress and in turn does that stress act as the trigger for migraine? No one really knows but, either way, migraines cost money.

The Statistics

- In the U.S. alone, approximately 112 million days are spent in bed every year as a result of migraines. The direct and indirect cost of this to the economy is believed to be $13 billion[65].
- 28 million people in the USA are estimated to suffer with migraine. Of these, 7 million will experience hunger as a migraine trigger[39].
- In a study[71] of 182 migraine patients in India, 87.9% reported specific triggers for their migraines. 34.4% of patients experienced more than two triggers. Emotional stress was a trigger for 70% of patients, fasting was a trigger for 46.3%, physical exhaustion or travelling was a trigger for 52.5%, sleep deprivation in 44.4%, menstruation in 12.8% and weather changes in 10.1%.
- One quarter of US households have a person who suffers with migraine[42].
- In a U.S. study[66], migraine prevalence was strongly associated with household income. Females aged between 30 and 49 yrs from lower income households were found to have a higher risk of migraine.
- Of those who seek medical care for their migraines, 72.2% will visit their primary care physician[25].
- Migraine commences earlier in males than females and migraine with aura starts earlier than migraine without aura in both males and females[43].
- In the U.S., the frequency of migraine attacks for men and women is similar. 25% of females who suffer with migraines experience on average, ≥ 4 severe attacks a month; 48% experience between 1 and 4 severe attacks each month and 38% experience ≤ 1 attack per month[42].
- Direct medical costs of migraine in the US are reported to be an estimated $11 billion per annum. This breaks down into $4.6 billion in prescription drugs, $5.2 billion for outpatient costs, $0.5 billion for ER and $0.7 billion for inpatient costs[32].
- Indirect costs associated with migraine include absenteeism, reduced productivity and short term disability[31].

Migraine Medication

(i)   Medication

Approximately 28 million Americans have migraines and of these, it is estimated that 14.8 million are severely restricted in their activities during migraine attacks[21]. Medication is typically prescribed for migraines and is often ef-fective. There are both ad-vantages and disadvan-tages with taking medica-tion. Irrespective of whether the medication is prophy-lactic (preventive) or abor-tive (stopping or interrupting a migraine attack), it can be expensive, and medication is rarely the perfect pana-  cea. If medication is your chosen path of management, the distinct advantage is that it will take less time to swallow a pill than to address an alternate way of managing migraines. However, as well as the expense, there is always a risk of becoming over-reliant on medication. The excessive consumption of analgesic (pain relieving) medications can also lead to further headaches, referred to as medication overuse headache, and this can make it more difficult to diagnose chronic migraine[68]. It is always useful to know what is available nonetheless.

(ii) Prophylactic Medication

Preventive, prophylactic medications which have been approved in the U.S. by the Food and Drug Administration are on a sliding scale of medications which have established efficacy right down to those which are probably ineffective. Research[60] has broken them down into categories according to their efficacy:

The drugs in the Level A box which satisfy their criteria for having established efficacy include:

   (1) Antiepileptic Drugs such as Topiramate
   (2) Beta blockers such as Timolol and Propanolol
   (3) Triptans such as Frovatriptan

One step down from these, there is a category of drugs which are deemed to be 'probably effective'. These include:

   1. Antidepressants/SSRI/SSNRI/TCA such as Amitriptyline
   2. Triptans such as Zolmitriptan

The drugs which are considered to have a *possible* role to play in preventing migraines include:

   1. Antihistamines such as Cyproheptadine
   2. ACE inhibitors such as Lisinopril

(iii) Abortive medications

For some people, migraine attacks are not frequent enough to warrant prophylactic medication. In such instances abortive medication might be prescribed. Some research[26] advises that when using abortive medications, they should be used as soon as possible once the migraine symptoms manifest. Triptans are considered first-line abortive treatment for moderate to severe migraine but as has been pointed out[26], complete pain relief is not always possible and these researchers note that the abortive medications are not advisable for anyone who has vascular problems. For milder migraines, the authors quote the U.S.

Headache Consortium guidelines which suggest the use of Non-Steroidal Anti-Inflammatory Drugs (NSAIDs) or caffeine containing combination analgesics. While these are the recommendations for acute treatment of migraine, in a study[8] examining 14,540 responses from individuals with episodic and chronic migraine, a pattern emerged to show that a considerable proportion are using medications which are not first-line according to the US Headache Consortium Guidelines. Of those with chronic migraine, 22% were using migraine-specific medications and more than 34% were using opiates or barbiturates. Of those with episodic migraine, 19.2% of subjects used migraine specific treatment, 11% used opiates and 6% used compounds with barbiturates.

Some questions to expect when attending your clinician for migraine intervention.

Although only a small percentage of people with migraine seek medical intervention, for those who actually do, the physician or neurologist is likely to ask many questions. There are usually two purposes behind their questions. The first is to find out the risk factors which are associated with your migraine, and the second is to address any other factors which may co-exist with the migraine, for example, depression or sleep related breathing disorders. The physicians will often enquire about the amount of caffeine you consume and the volume of pain killers you are taking. When obesity is a problem, it too may need to be addressed. Medication overuse can also be a problem and chances are high that the advice will be to cease the use of said medication. The inquisition is important. It allows the physician to develop a medical history and rule out other disorders such as brain tumour or stroke which may be causing the chronic head pain. When other underlying causes have been ruled out then a headache disorder can be considered.

Environment

"When the well's dry, we know the worth of water."
Benjamin Franklin

(i)   The weather

In Ireland, we talk about the weather constantly. Nice day... soft day....
mild day...miserable day.. The expressions are very much a part of our
daily discourse, and could be considered consequential with respect to
the unpredictability of our climate. To elaborate a little more and explain,
in Ireland, we have had frequent exposure to a non-sequitur sequence
of sunshine, showers, snow and storms all in one day. Temperatures
can plummet and rise dramatically with little heed to the weatherman's
warnings. If the ubiquitous anecdotal evidence about migraineurs and
environmental influences is correct however, then migraine sufferers
could probably save those who do not suffer from migraines the element
of surprise when it comes to predicting the weather.

(ii)   *Lights, smells and noise*

When environment is mentioned in conjunction with migraines, it often alludes to factors such as the weather, bright lights, odours, noise and air travel among other elements. Some migraineurs will complain that odours such as cigarette smoke will trigger their migraine. Others will cite humidity and flickering lights as the culprits instigating their pain. Few studies have directly investigated the effect of environmental factors on migraine but some of the studies which have  explored environment were reviewed in an article[22] published in 2009. The article describes a list of studies which illustrate the link between weather and barometric pressure changes, and the onset of migraine. However, it points out that when the migraine diaries on which some of the data is based are compared with weather reports, the effect of the weather may be over-estimated. The article suggests that other environmental factors such as pollution, exposure to chemicals and air quality may be partially responsible. In the same review, when the researchers looked at studies investigating the area of odours and migraine, they unearthed quite a few studies which found that odours were identified as a trigger in over 40% of migraineurs. They also note that osmophobia, which is an aversion to odours, is present in the same percentage of migraineurs. The review concludes with a sentiment which we will examine more in the part of this book entitled 'Stress –

thresholds', and notes that migraineurs are often more sensitive to specific stimuli in the environment and that this can lead to a deviation from normal activation in the cerebral cortex and brain stem.

> To manage your migraines effectively using the ProMigraine Programme, awareness of the environmental triggers personally affecting you is important.

(iii)   Social Situation

Environment matters. Two of our great modern architects, Frank Lloyd Wright and Ludwig Mies van der Rohe understood the fundamental impact of space on mood and on life. Frank Lloyd Wright conceived collections of open spaces in lieu of rooms. He thought in terms of design and individuality. He was also responsible for leading the Prairie school movement which encouraged and celebrated craftsmanship and rejected mass production lines, wholly considering them to be a source of unkindly human automation and ignominious ways. His contemporary, Ludwig Mies van der Rohe was interested in attention to detail, the preservation of dignity at all cost and the provision of simplicity and freedom for the benefactors of his architectural creations. Elegant simplicity, wide open spaces with room to breathe and consideration of each person as a unique being with accordingly personal preferences influenced much of the thinking which led to the creations of beautiful works of architecture which we are now so familiar with. Homage to our health need not necessarily stray too far beyond the thinking of these creative giants. While each of us is unique in our propensity to like or dislike any number of alternatives, the shared rules of simplicity and due diligent attention to those finer details and accessories exclusive to our genotypes must be considered and embraced in our own personal quests for peak physical health.

All things being equal, if you were to consider the place where you would be most at peace where would you find yourself? Would you choose to meander softly along Ave President Wilson as you explore the picturesque, Parisian markets for fine foods or would fighting your way through an alternate, ill planned, chaotic, disease and smog ridden city in search of sustenance satisfy your inner calm? Most of us will probably find greater solace in the beautiful French capital with its expansive boulevards and thoughtfully designed buildings where there is something new to observe at every turn. Along the beautiful boulevards some of us will linger, entranced by the activities of residents and tourists alike while others will be drawn into the colourful sights, smells and sounds of the busy market thoroughfare, oblivious to those around us. The commonalities and differences make us the same and also unique. These incomparable, multiplicitous layers of thinking, observing and being will always preserve our individuality and when common factors are also included in a game-plan, progress can be expedited.

Conveyer belts of hackneyed treatments and stereotyped tenets of thinking are unquestionably unfair to the unwitting patient. The solution, if you decide to allocate time to the process, is a combination of awareness and action. Once you are aware of yourself, your thinking and the situations in which you surround yourself then that awareness can be broadened to possibilities and the pursuit of action along the path most suited to your personal expectations and decided requirements.

Migraine triggers, including environmental factors, are often overlooked in the search for a better way to manage the chronic pain or in a rush to resume the 'normal working day'. To apply all aspects of the ProMigraine Programme it is important for each individual to examine all possible causes and triggers of migraine for themselves personally and consider the situational factors which affect one's physiology at a certain period in time. Armed with this knowledge it is then possible to create an effective, personal plan designed to minimise the adverse affect of migraines tailored specifically for you as an individual.

As humans we often adopt a sheepish attitude, blindly following the instructions of others who have some experience in the area.

Admittedly, when others have studied an area in depth and researched the various possibilities it can shorten our journey when seeking a solution to a problem. However, given the confusion over the specific aetiology of migraines and the fact that we all have different tolerance thresholds both on an inter-individual and intra-individual level, it makes sense to consider the impact of environment in our ProMigraine Management Programme.

Consider Milgram's obedience studies conducted at Yale University in 1961. Milgram was interested in testing just how far we will sacrifice our moral beliefs while answering to someone in a position of authority. An advert in a paper was used to recruit subjects who were then assigned to the task of 'teacher' or 'learner'. In reality, all subjects recruited were given the role of teacher and actors were assigned to the role of 'learner'. Both experimenter and teacher were assigned to one room, and the learner was allocated to another room where they were not visible to either experimenter or teacher. The role of the 'teacher' was to administer an electric shock of varying amplitude to the 'learner' each time they got a question wrong. The 'teachers' believed that their subjects were being given electric shocks and when they administered the shocks they would 'hear' the learner shriek in distress from the pain. In actuality, they were listening to a tape recorder which had been prepared with verbal responses corresponding to each 'shock' level administered. Although many of the 'teachers', believing their subjects to be in pain, requested to stop the experiment, after some verbal encouragement from the experimenter such as 'it is essential that you continue', many of the 'teachers' continued to administer shocks of increasing amplitude. The maximum shock which they could administer was a frighteningly high 450 volts. When a group of 40 psychiatrists were asked to assess how many 'teachers' would continue giving shocks up to the maximum level, the psychiatrists polled said they thought only one out of one thousand individuals would deliver that 450 volt shock. They were incorrect. The actual number of 'teachers' who went so far as to administer the 450 volt shock to their 'learners' for incorrect answers was a massive 65% of the 40 people who participated. There are many lessons to be learned from Milgrams experiments, including the fact that we are highly inclined to trust and follow individuals in positions of authority. Another lesson which became clear from the poll of psychiatrists is how easy it is for medically trained individuals to focus on disposition and to ignore situational influences. In doing so, something called the 'fundamental attribution error' was committed. This error highlights the tendency to over emphasise the role of personality and overlook the influence of environment and situation.

(iv) Perception, Thoughts, Behaviour and Physiology

Another experiment cited frequently to illustrate our acquiescence to authority is the Stanford Prison Experiment. Philip Zimbardo is a well known social psychologist and perhaps best known for his experiment conducted in 1971 and which has since been compared with the abuse of prisoners in Abu Ghraib Prison in Iraq in 2004. Students of Stanford University who agreed to take part in an experiment during the summer of 1971, designed to investigate the psychological effects of prison life. Those chosen to participate were randomly assigned either the role of prisoner or guard. After a dramatic 'arrest', those chosen to be prisoners were brought to a prison which was located in the Psychology building at Stanford University. Those allocated the role of guard were given batons to re-enforce their authority. The mock prisoners were stripped naked and searched and ultimately humiliated while being issued with a prison uniform, a prison ID number and being fitted with a chain and bolt around their ankle. The guards in this experiment were given carte blanche to administer any disciplinary action, within reason, that they deemed necessary to maintain law and order in the prison. The guards became increasingly forceful in their administration of punishment to the prisoners. Reality and drama merged and became increasingly difficult for both prisoners and guards to separate. Ultimately, the prisoners demonstrated behaviour which could only be described as subservient as they showed a distinct lack of power and an un-nerving lack of understanding between what was real (they were actors in an experiment) and what was perceived and felt (they were prisoners). Their findings showed no link between personality and behaviour within the mock prison situation with the exception that the participants with a naturally high propensity towards authoritarianism were able to survive longer in the experimental prison than those with a lower degree of authoritarianism. Those allocated the role of prisoners eventually showed pathological patterns of behaviour while the guards became willing conspirators in inducing feelings of hopelessness in their prisoners.

(v)   *Restore Balance*

One of the major lessons which the Stanford Prison Experiment teaches us is that, environment matters. It is important to be aware of how your working environment, your home environment and your social backdrop influence the frequency and intensity of your migraines. Then you can, in turn, consider potential changes which could reduce the severity levels and the duration of the migraine pain. Environment affects our behaviour which in turn affects our physiology. To restore balance, maintain homeostasis and avoid the neurasthenic symptoms of migraine, we need to examine our environment closely and coldly observe the schismatic influences which tear at our resources and deplete our reserves.

We will always pay more for something which is unique. Down through the ages painters, sculptors and architects have understood this concept. Highly prized works of art are valued because of their exclusiveness. They will cost much more than mass produced materials and their privilege lies somewhat in their selectiveness. A time investment  is required in the restoration of any health ailment and just as the discerning art collector may traipse from one art dealer to the next, using a sharp eye and a specific shopping list, your investment might be short or it may be long depending largely on the levels of insight gleaned from preparation, awareness and action. At this stage of your Promigraine

Programme you may wish to consider painting a picture of the life you would like to create going forward. Include the specifications which you consider to be minimal requirements in this part of your workbook. Then imagine you are an observer of your own environment and highlight the areas at home, socially and at work which are causing you stress or upsetting the balance you are striving for in each of those areas. There is also space in your workbook to identify solutions which could be applied. Often it can be as easy as changing your perception of the circumstances that you find yourself in. Other solutions may require more energy but, in the long run may hasten the journey to equilibrium and a life that has fewer migraines or none at all.

ELIMINATING TRIGGERS

Part II

Hormones and Migraines

(i)   Hormones and migraines

Hormones are known to influence the incidence and management of migraines. In a study[67] exploring the prevention of migraine in women, it was noted that menstruation, pregnancy, oral contraception, menopause and hormone therapy should be considered when devising a migraine management strategy. They point out that 60% of women who have migraines note that those migraines are related to their menstrual cycle and are likely to be migraine without aura. When oestrogen declines during the menstrual cycle, this can act as a trigger for migraine. The research also quotes a review by the International Headache Society Task Force on Combined Oral Contraceptives and Hormone Replacement Therapy which indicates that female migraineurs who experience aura or who present with other risk factors for stroke and who smoke and use combined oral contraceptives should be assessed very carefully. The combination of combined oral contraceptives, cigarette smoking and migraine increases the risk of stroke 34-fold. The study reports the curious fact that despite the high incidence of migraine amongst women and the debilitating effect it can have on day to day living, only 3-5% of women receive preventive therapy.

(ii)   Women and migraines.

Migraine is more common than diabetes, osteoarthritis or asthma. In fact, approximately 18% of women experience migraines and yet only 3% to 5% of them are in receipt of preventive therapy[67]. Women are approximately three times more likely than men to suffer with migraine. In fact, approximately 60% of female migraineurs have migraine attacks associated with their menstrual cycle particularly when oestrogen levels drop in the days prior to menstruation. Hormones clearly have a role to play in managing migraines. In terms of an overall management plan, identifying the days ahead of time can be useful. Once you have identified the migraine triggers which affect you the most, avoidance strategies will ideally be enforced with even more rigor during this time of the month. This might mean being even more mindful about your nutrition and the balance of minerals and vitamins you are taking or perhaps it could involve clearing part of your schedule so that you have time to meditate. Consulting a nutritionist may be very helpful in guiding you in the right direction due to the fact that specific foods will have an effect on our hormones. There is a school of thought which suggests that almost all hormonally-related health issues can be rectified with the correct nutrition. Nutrition alone may not be the panacea for migraine but as a part of the jigsaw its relevance should not be underestimated.

Nutrition

(i)   Food and drink

There is no disputing it. Research studies and anecdotal reports often cite nutrition as a precipitating factor to migraine. Alcohol, chocolate and cheese are three of the most frequently reported dietary triggers for migraine in sufferers. Even though the studies might dispute the actual percentage - anywhere between 12 and 60 % of patients, it is clear that diet matters[20] and should be an integral part of your migraine management programme.

(ii)   The role of Tyramine

For those who suffer with migraines, the finding that food and alcohol can be triggers for migraines is hardly a scientific breakthrough. Nevertheless, the means by which the nutritional trigger exerts its effect is still an enigma. One theory revolves around Tyramine. Tyramine is released in food when the amino acid tyrosine is naturally broken down. It is often attributed with migraine provoking properties. The levels of Tyramine increase in food that is aged, fermented or stored for a long time. Fermented soya products such as Miso soup, alcohol and aged cheeses such as cheddar cheese often contain high levels of Tyramine. A study published by The Lancet in 1988 looked into the matter further, by giving their patients a cold drink in a dark bottle. Some of the patients were given red wine and some were given vodka with a mix. Both drinks contained the same volume of alcohol. The researchers found that even though the red wine had a negligible amount of Tyramine, nine of the 11 participants suffered a migraine attack while none of the 8 who consumed the vodka had an attack. The researchers concluded that something other than the alcohol and the Tyramine content of the red wine is responsible for provoking migraine.

(iii)   Food intolerance

Other research[59] has even suggested that the 'food allergy' which patients describe is nothing more than a psychological response to a particular food itself. Even though the author of the latter research dismisses elimination diets, they conclude their article by advising migraine patients to consume alcohol with caution, to avoid large amounts of monosodium glutamate, aspartame and perhaps cured meat. In the meantime, while academics argue, patients continue to suffer. Whether or not dietary related migraine is precipitated by physiological or psychological mechanisms, if identification and elimination help to decrease the frequency and intensity of migraines, then it is a worthy inclusion in a migraine management plan.

(iv)   Phenylethylamine, histamine and other compounds

Compounds such as phenylethylamine, histamine, nitrates and sulphites have also been singled out[49] for their contributory part in food intolerance headache. The theory behind this is that dietary triggers influence the various stages of the migraine process either by influencing the release of serotonin and norepinephrine, thereby causing vasoconstriction or vasodilation or by direct stimulation of the brainstem and other pathways. One problem with studying food or alcohol as triggers is measuring the quantity of particular foods ingested and their relation, if any, to other triggers such as weather or travel and/or stress. What is important for your own ProMigraine programme is whether you can identify a pattern of particular foods or drinks which precipitate an attack for you personally.

Although the search for particular agents within foods and drinks that are guilty of triggering migraines is on-going and the dispute as to whether the dietary triggers are all in one's head or have a valid physiological basis persists, consideration of all elements to reduce or eliminate migraines is important. Once you identify a pattern of specific foods, if any, which provoke a migraine attack, you can progress your migraine management plan one step further. This is a personal plan which you are designing for yourself and what is effective for you may vary considerably from other migraine sufferers that you know.

(v)   Low Fat Diets

Thanks to the ubiquitous bombardment of messages from medics and media alike you are probably familiar with the many benefits of a low fat diet. Did you know however that a low fat diet is also beneficial for managing your migraines? One study[7] involved 54 migraine patients aged between 24 and 71 years in a study who were asked to follow a low fat diet. After reducing the fat content of their diet the results were very positive. In addition to having fewer migraines, the migraines they did have were less intense. They had lost weight, lowered their body fat percentages and blood lipids as well. The authors point out that because the diet change was dramatic, there was an accompanying change in the nutrients which the participants were consuming. They also note that lower circulating free fatty acids and other blood lipid levels will affect serotonin levels so they cannot categorically say that the outcome is solely due to a low fat diet. Either way, the diet had many benefits for participants and could be considered as an option for anyone whose diet is currently high in fat content. If you do decide to embark on a low fat diet as part of your programme it might be helpful to know that the overall fat grams in the study dropped from an average of 65.9g per day to 27.8g per day. It takes time to change ones diet and to find alternative foods which will satisfy your tastes and your lifestyle so patience and advice from a nutritionist could save a lot of unwarranted stress along the way.

(vi)   Supplements

Anecdotal reports and academic research have unearthed certain natural supplements which are helpful in some cases. The use of magnesium has been recommended[24] to reduce migraine frequency and severity, and there are reasons to believe that fish oils in large quantities may have the same effect. 'Feverfew', a natural herb which looks very similar to daisies, is also well known to many migraineurs as an effective treatment to reduce headache frequency, nausea and vomiting.

(vii)   Fasting

28 million people in the USA alone suffer with migraine and of these it is estimated that 7 million will experience hunger as a migraine trigger[39]. This statistic alone should be enough to encourage even the busiest migraine patient to ensure they have a regular intake of food at all times. Chances are that sometimes the connection between hunger and migraine is overlooked or priority is given to important tasks in the hope that migraine will stay away. The researchers point out that the pathophysiology of fasting-induced headache is still not fully understood but may be due to an effect on fatty acid metabolism. They also point out that there is some evidence to suggest that lack of water for a lengthy period can also act as a trigger for migraine. As part of your personal plan it is worth making a note of any meals you have missed preceding a migraine or whether you have not consumed water for an increased period of time. If these are the primary connections for triggering migraines in your life then prevention is easy. Chances are that there are a few other triggers but by narrowing it down to those which affect you most and implementing the appropriate, practical steps, you could dramatically reduce or even eliminate those pesky migraines.

Stress

(i)   Emotional thresholds

Stress can be useful –
sometimes. At other
times, it can be toxic.
Occasionally, it may
even seem as though
the factors contributing
to our stress are outside
of our control. Before
playing the blame game
however, and angrily
lashing out at the impu-
dence of the universe
and all within it, it might
be useful to consider the

wise words of Benjamin Graham in his formidable magnum opus, 'The
Intelligent Investor'. The undisputed authority on value investing in the
stock market remarks; "The fault dear investor, is not in our stars – and
not even in our stocks – but in ourselves". Good counsel for all areas of
life whether or not you are interested in making money on the stock
market or managing your migraines. Throughout life we will be
presented with a series of choices. We can anticipate the outcome of
our decisions to a point but most of the time we will have to hedge our
bets. It does not always work out. Nevertheless we always have a
choice and with choice comes responsibility. Ultimately, this is a positive
thing as it means we retain control and as such we can reverse or
amend our decisions and subsequently alter the outcome.

For migraine patients, management of stress is essential. In fact, stress and mental tension have been singled out as the most conspicuous precipitating factor in migraines and tension type headaches[53]. When the body and mind are in a state of flux, regression to homeostasis is vital. For healing to occur, restoring balance needs to be a priority. The first step here is to acknowledge your limits. Two people in the same situation will most likely perceive that situation differently. Imagine for example that you are one of a hundred people going into a movie theatre to watch a well publicized movie. On your way out you encounter a researcher who is asking you what you thought of the movie. On this occasion imagine that you happen to have enjoyed the movie but feel that it fell somewhat short of your expectations so you rate it as being 'OK'. You ask the researcher what the other people thought of the movie and she explains that 30% thought it was fantastic, another 30% thought it was terrible and the remaining 40% thought it was just OK. You reflect on the thinking behind this. After all, all one hundred people saw the exact same film. What each person thought of it was most likely not a true reflection of what it actually was. The perception was indeed filtered by life experience, likes, dislikes, expectations and a host of other variables.

When dealing with stress, some of us are a very relaxed bunch of individuals and can deal with an inordinate volume of tasks and demands. The remainder are often better focusing on one task at a time. Furthermore, the nature of the demands will vary from person to person. Everyone, it would appear, develops their own skills set and comfort zone. While some people are very happy to explore beyond their comfort zones, for others it is a sure fire way to feel psychological stress which in turn can lead to undesirable and unpleasant increases in physiological stress markers. Psychological tolerance levels and physiological pain thresholds vary from person to person and throughout one's lifetime. At any specific moment in time, the set point of these thresholds depends, most probably, on a mixture of environmental influences, perception, genetics and conditioning.

What may be useful for the migraineur in terms of managing the pain, is to determine one's own personal, emotional threshold. Once the limits have been established and communicated to all and sundry, changes in the demands on your time and the use of your skills can be revisited and restructured as necessary. And of course, given that the world is populated with people of many persuasions, there will be those who will aim to push those boundaries from time to time. These, essentially, are individuals who are either lacking in social perspicacity and emotional insight or are inflicted with an unenviable narcissistic disposition. Thus, the company you surround yourself with might be worth considering also.

(ii) Health consequences of psychological and physiological stressors on migraine

While the experimental evidence documenting the impact of stress on migraines in particular is severely lacking, evidence abounds regarding the impact of psychological and physiological stress on health. Research crossing medical, psychological and physiological disciplines has long held the view that amplified responses to stress for example, contribute to an increased risk of cardiovascular disease[45]. The immune system is also vulnerable to the ravages of stress. For example, in the area of autoimmune disease, up to 80% of patients report uncommon emotional stress before the onset of disease[64]. There is no shortage of studies illustrating the fact that stress causes disease.

Prior to a migraine, migraineurs have been shown to have a significantly increased response to stress as measured by neurophysiological activity, that is, activity of the nervous system, when compared with individuals who do not suffer with migraines[61]. In the study which documents this, the physiological stress indicators under stressful conditions were more pronounced in migraine patients, particularly one to three days prior to an attack. What this actually means is that the brain of a migraine patient is more susceptible to migraine triggers before an actual attack occurs. The theory these scientists subscribe to is that a migraine attack will occur in one of two instances: The first is when a migraine trigger is present and is strong enough to elicit the attack and the second is when the trigger is not particularly strong but the attack threshold in the brain is lowered. This study indicates that the causes of changes in the attack threshold in the brain of a migraine patient are as of yet elusive. Nevertheless, once external triggers are identified, awareness alone is a useful tool in the migraine manager toolbox and forms much of the basis of your ProMigraine Programme.

(iii)   Identifying the stressors in your life

The natural corollary is to sit down and identify the current stressors in your life and then redesign your life so that you can eliminate them, amend them or perceive them differently. Over time you could also keep a track of all stressful events and experiences which you face and note whether you had a migraine during or shortly after those events and experiences. If there is something you can't do but you feel you should be able to do because your neighbour down the road can do it, don't beat yourself up over it. Stress induced by feelings of failure is futile. We all have different strengths and weaknesses. You might excel in a different area where your neighbour would struggle. The world needs a mix of skills. One man (or woman) alone cannot build a motorway. It takes architects, builders, engineers; an entire team. Find your strengths and capitalise on them. Find your weaknesses and research how best to provide support for those areas or choose a different path to get to the same destination. The choice, just like the responsibility, is yours.

Whether you believe that it does or believe that it doesn't act as a trigger for migraines, stress management is clearly an integral part of any worthy optimal health programme and, with a little time and thought, can be implemented within a reasonable time frame.

Sleep

"I dream my painting and I paint my dream."

Vincent Van Gogh

(i)   Effects of sleep deprivation

Engaging in dreams while awake and asleep is a necessity not an indulgence. Thus, if sleep is evading you, then pay close attention. Sleep is one of our most basic human needs. Maslow placed it on the

axiological rung of his hierarchy of needs along with food, hunger and thirst. We complain if we don't have enough of it and often delight when able to avail of the occasional morning where there is an excess of it.

Deprivation of this basic human need has, historically, been widely used as an effective torture technique in prison camps to force confessions from prisoners. Whatever your belief is about Darwinian philosophies and our place in the taxonomic ranks of the biological classification systems, what we know from a study by Allan Rechtschaffen in Chicago is that sleep is essential for us to survive. His study found that enforced, long-term sleep deprivation in rats led to death. There are several theories about the changes instigated by the sleep deprivation in these rats as to whether it was the drop in body temperature of the rats', changes in their immune system or something else. Irrespective of the persistent impact and subsequent changes, the rats died. Sleep is important. Clearly it is neither ethical nor moral to perform such experiments on humans, and where sleep deprivation is actively inflicted the findings will rarely be reported. In such instances of moral dilemmas and the pursuit of answers, our understandings rely on retrospective musings. One such unfortunate discovery arose during Euro 2012 when it was reported that a Chinese soccer fan died from exhaustion after staying up for eleven consecutive nights to watch all of the European Championship games. Sleep deprivation exerts adverse psychological and physiological consequences on its victims, and unless you have placed other engagements higher on your priority of needs scale, then sufficient sleep may be one pleasant active agent along your path to successful migraine management.

(ii)   How much sleep is enough for migraineurs?

The fact that the relationship between migraines and sleep is a hazy one is not all that surprising. Despite advances in science, we are scratching the surface in terms of our understanding of sleep itself. How much sleep is optimal? How do we measure the units of sleep? Should we rely on the sleep deprivation paradigm to enlighten us about sleep itself and should sleep be measured in units of time or in terms of NON-REM/REM cycles[70]. There are many unanswered questions about sleep. Nevertheless, in the context of migraines what we do know is that sleep is important. While we do not fully understand *why* it is important, research has indicated that migraine is positively associated with many sleep-complaint disorders such as restless-leg syndrome. Furthermore, questions have been raised about the association between migraines and insomnia, snoring and sleep apnea[14]. It is somewhat of a chicken and egg situation. Which comes first? Does migraine lead to problems where one finds it difficult to fall asleep or stay asleep (insomnia) or problems where there is an excessive sleepiness and extended sleep time (hypersomnia) or do these issues play a causative role in the development of migraines?

Scientific research can be useful but dispersion of the findings in a way that can be understood by those with no scientific background and practical application of the findings often fails to follow. One study[13] which did look at the subjective impact that sleep deprivation had on its participants, asked patients to report whether they awoke 'feeling refreshed' or 'tired'. Of the 147 women who took part in the study not one of them reported awakening 'refreshed' and 83.7% said that they woke up feeling tired. The researchers concluded that sleep complaints were commonplace and assorted.

Another study which was conducted a few years earlier, uncovered similar findings. Sleep complaints are common among migraineurs. This earlier study[37] evaluated 1,283 migraineurs and assessed variables such as sleep and demographics. Over half of the participants, all of whom suffered with migraines, found it difficult either getting to sleep or staying asleep. The irony of the findings in this study was that sleep was seen as a palliative agent for their headache with 75% of the migraineurs saying that they had no choice but to sleep or rest because of the pain. The people who suffered with chronic migraine, that is, migraine on 15 or more days each month, were classified as 'short sleepers'. This refers to the fact that they routinely slept an average of six hours in twenty four. Those who slept more were more likely to be episodic migraineurs i.e. they had fewer migraines. A study published in the Lancet in 1977 measured a number of physiological markers such as tryptophan, glucose and free fatty acids in a group of 19 migraine sufferers who awoke regularly from sleep with a migraine. They also made polygraph sleep recordings and found that when the migraineurs woke from sleep it was predominantly during REM sleep[34]. Among the many functions of REM sleep, consolidation of procedural memory is associated with this phase of slumber. Procedural memory pertains to how we perform activities. So, if you were a pianist and you had learned a new piece, REM sleep will help you to consolidate and recall the movement of your hands across the piano. REM sleep also aids in preserving emotional memories.

Keep it simple...

Ensure you are providing the right environment, inside and outside of your body to ensure you are getting sufficient quality sleep.

FACTORS INFLUENCING YOUR SUCCESS

Part III

Natural Remedies For Migraine

Feverfew, Riboflavin and Magnesium are three popular over-the-counter remedies often used to treat migraine.

(i)   Feverfew

Feverfew is a member of the daisy family and has found its own dedicated fan base in the world of migraine sufferers. In the same way one person might have a preference for fried food and another for grilled, our physiological response to medicine and herbs and can differ and will be affected by a number of factors. Some people who have used feverfew have experienced no side effects. Other users of feverfew have reported skin rash and sore mouth as a consequence of taking the herb. Currently, the anecdotal reports of its efficacy outweigh the scientific reports but there are a limited number of studies available which have investigated the prophylactic effects of feverfew. One such study gave 48 patients a compound which contained a mixture of 400mg of riboflavin, 100mg of feverfew and 300mg of magnesium or a placebo. It was a double blind study meaning that neither the researchers nor the patients were told whether they had a placebo or the active compound. The placebo contained 25mg of riboflavin. Both groups showed significant improvement in terms of the number of migraines and the number of migraine days, and also the migraine index. Given that the placebo response in this study was larger than that of other migraine prophylactic studies, the researchers concluded that 25mg of riboflavin was an effective prophylactic in its own right and both placebo and active compound were useful for patients in this instance. Following publication of this study, a letter to the journal 'Headache', suggested that the study was flawed and that one of the limitations was that the feverfew dosage in the active compound was too low to be effective. Nevertheless, countless stories inhabit the internet about the powerful effect of this plant. Therefore if natural herbs are your preferred prophylactic then feverfew may be worth investigating in greater detail. A herbalist will have a great deal of information about how this non-conventional treatment may help you and they might even be able to sell you some seeds so that you can grow the herb yourself.

> When a migraine is starting, the serotonin levels rise and the blood vessels start to constrict. Feverfew and Magnesium are believed to trigger a chain of events which cause the blood vessels to dilate thus counteracting the constriction.

(ii)   Riboflavin

Riboflavin (Vitamin B2) is a water soluble vitamin so we cannot store it in our bodies. Hence we need to ensure we eat foods which contain riboflavin every day. It is involved in red blood cell production, increasing energy levels and a host of other functions. It is found in milk, eggs and green vegetables among other foods. For migraineurs, a supplement of riboflavin, usually of 400mg, has been found to be very useful in reducing the number of migraine attacks experienced.

In one study[10] involving 23 patients (6 of whom had migraine with aura and 17 who had migraine without aura), patients were given a capsule each day which contained 400mg of riboflavin. The 400mg of riboflavin was successful in reducing the number of migraine attacks that patients had and the study also found that the headache duration was decreased from 50 hours in the month prior to taking riboflavin to 28 hours a month in the third and sixth month of taking riboflavin. This latter decrease was not statistically significant however, and no reduction in the severity (intensity) of the headache was observed. The use of abortive drugs decreased in this study from 7 units a month to 4.5 units a month. Therefore, while riboflavin may assist in reducing the number of migraine attacks and the number of abortive migraine drugs being consumed, in this instance it did not have an effect on the severity of migraine.

The way in which riboflavin works was investigated by researchers[55] who found that it has a different effect on the body than betablockers would exert. Both betablockers and riboflavin have effective prophylactic properties for migraineurs but the pathways by which both work are different. Betablockers can have an adverse effect on the central nervous system while riboflavin, they explain, is very well tolerated. It works by improving mitochondrial energy metabolism, a factor which can be compromised in migraineurs. Betablockers, on the other hand, work by exerting a change in information processing in the cortex in the brain so that normal cortical information processing is restored. This can, they say, involve a change in neuronal excitability or a change in neurotransmitter activity, or both. They conclude that the reason riboflavin does not seem to have side effects on the CNS is that the positive changes in mitochondrial function are not accompanied by changes in neuronal excitability.

Riboflavin side effects are rare. One study[57] which did report side effects used the same amount of riboflavin (400mg) as the previous study when they divided their group of 55 patients into a placebo group and a riboflavin treatment group. Diarrhoea and polyuria (excessive passage of volume of urine) were reported by two of their twenty eight patients who were in the riboflavin treatment group. Interestingly, in this study too, riboflavin was found to be an effective migraine prophylactic and while 15% of the placebo group improved in terms of experiencing fewer migraine attacks, 59% of the riboflavin group also experienced fewer attacks. Within the placebo group one of the patients reported abdominal pain. The researchers concluded that riboflavin is an interesting option for keeping migraines at bay given that it is highly effective, tolerated well by most patients and it is inexpensive.

(iii)   Magnesium

Magnesium is one of those minerals we need for a myriad of reasons. Our sources of magnesium include green vegetables, whole grains and water but there are many others. Approximately half of the magnesium in your body will be stored in your bones. The other half is divided

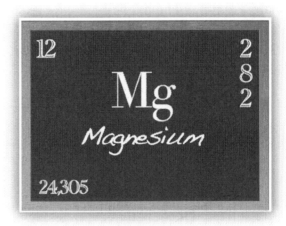

between the cells in the body and the blood, although only a tiny amount (approximately 1%) is carried in the blood. Magnesium has a multitude of responsibilities in the body including maintaining healthy nerve and muscle tissue function, regulating blood sugar levels and preventing diseases such as cardiovascular disease and diabetes. Even by consuming a healthy diet which is rich in foods that are good sources of magnesium we can sometimes inadvertently become magnesium deficient. Deficiency can be caused by taking certain medications, for example antibiotics, or because of poor absorption of minerals due to Crohn's disease. Old age can also affect absorption of magnesium.

Magnesium deficiency is believed to play a part in the pathogenesis of migraine for many individuals. In fact, up to 50% of migraineurs may be magnesium deficient[46]. This study source for this statistic quotes two other studies which found magnesium to be an effective prophylactic for migraineurs. In both studies neither patients nor consultants knew (double-blind) whether they were being treated with magnesium or placebo. A third study did not find magnesium effective but the authors suggest that in this instance it could be due to poor absorption of the mineral as a result of the preparation used and they suggest that chelated magnesium is one of the better absorbed preparations. Their recommendations for chelated magnesium diglycinate are 600mg/day. In a more recent study, researchers suggested that magnesium is effective in particular in treating patients who have migraine with aura as it is effective in treating photophobia and phonophobia. They also note that magnesium is safe to use during pregnancy[36].

There are many variables which will influence measurement in studies so all results must be interpreted with caution. It has also been highlighted[46] that much of the scepticism surrounding the use of magnesium supplementation for migraine could be due to many factors, among them, how magnesium deficiency is assessed. To give you an example of how findings can be flawed, these researchers[46] recommend using serum ionised magnesium level rather than total serum or intracellular levels of the ion.

(iv) Phytotherapy

Phytotherapy is the use of herbs and/or plants for medicinal purposes. Chinese medicine has a different approach to medicine compared with orthodox Western medicine. The exhaustive list which could be compiled when comparing both is beyond the scope of this chapter and indeed this book. Suffice it to say, I think it is reasonable to surmise that Eastern medicine, in its approach to restore health, considers the balance between the spirit, mind and body while the main focus of Western medicine is to alleviate pain and treat symptoms. Lifestyle is considered a major part of Eastern medicine and while it is gaining some stature among a proportion of medics who practice Western medicine, the fact remains that treatment is still heavily reliant on alleviating physical symptoms. Both approaches to medicine can be helpful and a consideration of both may be even more powerful in prevention and treatment. Traditional Chinese medicine believes that migraine is due to the pathogenic wind-cold, blood stasis and failure in nourishing and it has been suggested[40] that Tou Feng Yu (TFY) pill, is a useful traditional Chinese herbal medicine for migraines. The authors explain that it is formulated from three herbs, Baizhi, Chuanxiong and green tea. The authors cite studies which demonstrate that Chuanxiog and Baizhi have a duplicitous effect in terms of exerting an analgesic effect, alleviating muscle spasm and improving abnormal blood flow, and Chuanxiong and green tea have proven cardio-cerebrovascular benefits. In their study, the researchers found that TFY had an anti-migraine effect through regulation of neurotransmitter levels, neuropeptides and other bioactive substances. This had the impact of alleviating neurogenic inflammation and restoring equilibrium. They recommend consideration of TFY as a means of supporting conventional drugs in the treatment of migraines.

(v)   Other complimentary treatments

Increasingly, people are turning to complimentary treatments as an adjunct or as an alternative to orthodox medicine for the treatment of migraines. Osteopathy, massage, cranio-sacral therapy, spinal manipulative therapy (SMT), homeopathy and acupuncture are just a few of the therapies which fall into this category. The aim of these treatments will vary but suffice it to say that, in general the aim of these therapies is to treat the body as a whole rather than solely treating the symptoms that present. Given the growing number of therapies available this could involve any number of approaches. If you feel that muscle tension for example is a contributing factor to your migraines it may be worth considering a trip to your osteopath or acupuncturist.

Exercise

"If we could give every individual the right amount of nourishment and exercise, not too little and not too much, we would have found the safest way to health."

Hippocrates

(i)   Exercise for health

I had the great privilege of working in the fitness industry as a gym instructor for many years. It was, without doubt, my favourite job of all time. After qualifying with the first ever group of gym instructors in Ireland, direct employment was scarce and the potential to develop a business was at its peak. There was one gym in my home city of Galway, Ireland which was largely high-jacked by 'intimidating' bodybuilders and shrouded by the common perception that it was a place to avoid if you lacked sufficient knowledge about creatine, human growth hormone, pyramid sets and barbells. In reality, it was a highly specialised fitness centre with the bare necessities in terms of equipment and a vision before its time. Perceptions about exercise when it comes to migraine can be confusing. We are told that severe physical exertion can exacerbate or initiate a migraine on one hand and that exercise is an excellent prophylaxis on the other hand. Bottom line is that exercise is beneficial and, in the correct dose, the benefits can be enormous. Exercise can improve brain function and cardiovascular fitness. It has a positive effect on our mood, it can help stave off neurodegenerative diseases such as Alzheimers and if your chosen exercise is a club based or team based activity it can be a great social hub. As someone whose world revolved around sport and exercise for a long time, it still amazes me that there are individuals who are simply unmoved by the joys and the benefits associated with exercise. Nevertheless, I have learned that there are horses for courses and that the world would be a very dull place if we all had the same likes and dislikes.

(ii)   Exercise for migraineurs

If you are a fan of sport and exercise and a migraine sufferer to boot then you are in luck because exercise has been shown to be beneficial in reducing the frequency[69] and severity[18] of migraine attacks. Aerobic exercise which is challenging enough to lead to a better fitness level has also been shown to be an alternative therapy method for migraine[18]. The associated onset of migraine can be avoided by doing a proper warm up and increasing activity slowly[23]. Recommendations from less recent studies are confusing. A review[12] of the literature prior to 2008 for example casts doubt on whether exercise was actually beneficial in reducing migraines, pre-dominantly due to study design issues and conflicting results. However, another study published the same year (2008) specifically measured the VO_{2max} of 26 migraine patients. VO_{2max} is a measure used to assess fitness levels and essentially measures the volume of oxygen used per kilogram of body weight per minute. The higher the VO_{2max}, the higher the cardiovascular fitness level. There was no deterioration in patients' migraines, and the researchers found that patients cardiovascular fitness improved and they also experienced a significant improvement in their quality of life. Admittedly, the scientific literature in the area of exercise and migraines is sparse and results from studies are confusing to say the least. So while the jury is out on exactly how exercise can affect frequency, severity or duration of migraine attacks, exercise is unlikely to have a negative effect and for the activity conscious individual, exercise offers a great opportunity to enjoy many other benefits which can, in and of themselves, be worth their weight in gold.

(iii)   Trust your instincts – and your gym instructor

I am a great believer in being subjective when it comes to exercise and while I appreciate the importance of scientific research, we each have our own unique patterns, environments, belief systems and personalities. While in college at the University of Sheffield I came across a system which rated perceived exertion during exercise. It confirmed my belief that we are often very proficient at assessing our own realities. The Borg scale is a psychophysiological scale which measures perceived exertion during exercise or training. The scale used can range from 0 to 10 or from 6 to 20.

This deceptively simple scale correlates with heart rate, blood lactate levels, ventilation and respiration rates and VO_{2max}. Research[16] that analysed the results of 64 studies which had examined the validity of Borg Scale found that there is a very definite correlation between how hard we perceive exercise to be and what the actual physiological tests will show us. There are a few variables which will influence the strength of the association, for example athletes who are highly trained tend to be more accurate in their rating. The bottom line is that whether you are a highly trained athlete or not, all of this research bodes well for our ability to judge our own physiology and to trust our own instinct. Combine this with a good education and advice from all quarters we are then in a better position to devise a plan which is unique to ourselves. Advice from an experienced gym instructor or sport psychologist could also save you a lot of time in the long run. They will be able to advise you what heart rate zone you should train in so that you are working at an intensity which can help you achieve your goals. They can also help you keep on track by varying your exercise programme every six to eight weeks. This will benefit both mind and for body. In essence, exercise, just like many other areas of your programme, requires education, adaptation, application and adherence. With due diligence, for many individuals, exercise may well be the most enjoyable and effective part of their ProMigraine Programme.

Time Management

"You cannot do a kindness too soon, for you never know how soon it will be too late."

Ralph Waldo Emerson

(i)   Migraines at what cost?

There is an opportunity cost with every decision we make. We can choose to stay within familiar patterns and be relatively sure of the outcome while intermittently whinging about how terrible particular aspects of our life happen are. Alternatively, we can identify the areas contributing to stress in our life, reassess the cost-effectiveness of those areas and redesign the relationships around them and within them. Take the ambitious business man or woman who juggles five different enterprises, flies all over the world and who, because of perceived lack of time to find a solution, is prepared to suffer intermittently with chronic migraine. When asked to list their priorities and values, their responsibility to hundreds of staff and the need to preserve their self-identity as a successful entrepreneur may be prioritised over and above the time set aside to take

care of health. The question of whether the time they could save if they had fewer hours devoured by being confined to bed with migraines simply never arises.. how could it.. the financial, social and personal outcomes are already identifiable and familiar.... You don't need to be a successful, jet-setting entrepreneur to find yourself in a pattern which, while it may satisfy many goals in your life, leaves your health in a less than desirable state.

(ii)   A cost-benefit analysis of your time

Once you have armed yourself with as much information about migraines as you require and you have completed your ProMigraine Programme workbook you should have a reasonably good idea of how much time you are going to set aside each month to manage your migraines and how much extra time, previously taken over by migraines, you will gain as a result of this investment. For those who find hypnosis beneficial, for example, it may be that listening to one fifteen minute migraine management hypnosis recording twice a week can reduce your migraine frequency by half and significantly reduce the severity, recouping hours, and sometimes days every single month. Thirty minutes each week to recover 24 hours. That has to be time well spent.

(iii)   Changing times

In an attempt to conserve time we all fall into patterns of behaviour. When productive, these patterns are essential for time management and for allocation of cognitive resources in the brain to pursue progression in areas which have been prioritised. When unproductive, our nodding acquaintance with these paradigms and prototypical patterns of behaviour allow us, grudgingly, to accept ill health and varying degrees of unhappiness as the natural order of things. We don't have to accept things as they are. Indeed, we would not progress though life if we did. What we do need to do however is stand back on occasion from the minutia and re-assess the broader brush-strokes. In the words of Abraham Lincoln, 'nothing valuable can be lost by taking time'. A good friend of mine who runs a successful business in Galway, Ireland, calls it 'quality dossing time'. Both Mr. Lincoln and my wonderful friend are both referring to the time set aside to allow the brain to process the whole picture and the series of events surrounding any given scenario. Knee jerk reactions often provoke a sequence of events which consume more time to amend in retrospect than the time which would have been consumed had a little thought and patience been invested from the start.

There are times when we all take on more than we are capable of handling. Whether deliberate or inadvertent, when overload occurs and the stress becomes less and less tolerable, it is time to cut the cloth or face the consequences. Undertaking the former can result in damage limitation and paradigmatic repercussions. Subscribing to the latter simply delays the inevitable cloth cutting and often results in a rather abrupt termination and a less than optimal outcome. How often have you heard of someone who drove themselves to the limit physically and mentally to the point where they ended up with an illness which rendered them unable to function at a fraction of the speed with which they operated to prior to their declension. There would seem to be some sense in the counsel to work intelligently as opposed to working hard.

Hypnosis and Migraines

"To stop an animal from moving forward in the course laid out for it by its natural instincts you have at least to hit it on the head with something hard. To obtain the same result with man you only have to talk to him."

Friedrich Nietzche

(i)   The power of words

An athlete I was working with recently, briskly remarked at the beginning of his second consultation 'You don't need to do the hypnosis part, that's just you talking.' He was correct. However, at the same time, he also fundamentally failed to grasp the incredible potency of words and the phenomenal power of the hypnotic state. Words have the ability to hurt. They also have the ability to heal. Choose the words you use wisely. Hypnosis is all about the use of words and semantics. Words are used to induce trance and words which are heard in a state of trance are significantly more powerful than those heard in the waking state. The former, specious nature of hypnosis has only now been validated by imaging techniques such as Magnetic Resonance Imaging (MRI) and Positron Emission Tomography (PET). Apart from improving our understanding of how words affect the physiology of the brain both in and out of trance, these scientific snapshots facilitate the potential to provide an insight into how one can further manipulate the potency of hypnotic intervention.

One research study[50] conducted in 2011 examined the way in which analgesic suggestions given to low back pain patients would alter the physiological processes in the brain. They found that during hypnosis, both analgesic suggestions of the direct and the indirect variety were equally successful in decreasing pain intensity by 64%. In the group who were not hypnotized, only the direct suggestions were effective and even then the decrease in pain intensity was a mere 20%. Although direct analgesic suggestions were effective in both normal alertness and hypnotic conditions, the results confirm the increased efficacy of hypnosis on pain modulation in the hypnotic state. A significant finding of this functional imaging study was that different networks in the brain were activated depending on whether the suggestions were given in the hypnotic state or in normal alertness. For those in the group who were not hypnotized, (normal alertness) the parts of the brain which deal with problem solving, attention, and decision making (cognitive network) and the parts of the brain which deal with intensity and location of pain (sensory network) were activated. In the hypnotic state, the same analgesic suggestions activated an emotional weighted network. Before considering hypnosis as a potential intervention for your migraines and given the fact that awareness is an integral part of any management plan for migraines, I have included further information about the topic of hypnosis in this chapter. Having spent many years working with hypnosis for a variety of ailments I have had the privilege of meeting and working with many wonderful people who were intent on creating incredible results. Their intentions rarely disappointed. Hypnosis is an interactional process. It requires skill on the part of the hypnotist and positive motivation on the part of the client.

(ii)   Hypnosis vs placebo

As a child I was taught never to assume anything and to keep an open mind. The advice has served me well and may well be responsible for my unquenching thirst for knowledge about just about every subject matter. Working with hypnosis for ten years was both a privilege and an education and finally science is catching up with the knowledge which practitioners of hypnosis have been espousing for years. Hypnosis is not a placebo. In fact, although testimonies of the power of hypnosis abound, the physiological markers of hypnosis have only recently been measured and perhaps for those not on the receiving or delivery end of hypnosis it may have been reasonable to assume that placebo and hypnosis were one and the same. A placebo, in medical settings, is an inert substance given to a patient who is led to believe that it has an active ingredient to alleviate pain or discomfort. PET scans have shown that the exact same pathways are activated in the brain by both placebo and an opiod drug, and furthermore when a substance designed to block a placebo analgesic response, e.g. Naloxone, is administered, it is successful in preventing the pain relief which would otherwise would have ensued as a result of the placebo[4]. This does not occur with hypnosis. That is to say that when hypnotic analgesia (as opposed to placebo analgesia) is utilised, naloxone is not effective in blocking the pain relief which occurs following analgesic suggestions given during hypnosis[63]. It is therefore reasonable to assume that hypnosis works on a very different physiological basis to placebo.

The extent of the power of words was demonstrated very clearly in an article[4] which recalls an experiment where post operative oral surgery patients were divided into two groups. One group were openly given an injection of what they perceived to be morphine but which was actually a placebo and the other group were given 6 to 8 mg of morphine by way of a hidden injection so they did not know when the painkiller was being injected. Both had the same pain-relieving effect, leading the researchers to surmise that telling the patient that they are receiving six to eight miligrams of morphine (when it was actually a placebo) was as powerful as an actual 6 to 8 mg injection of morphine. The researchers only noticed an increased analgesic effect when the hidden morphine dose was increased to 12 mg.

(iii)   The power of hypnosis

We now have concrete proof that the words spoken while administering a placebo are important. We have seen also from the study on patients wtih back pain that hypnotic suggestions can be up to three times more powerful than suggestions given without hypnosis. Despite this knowledge, some stigma and miconceptions prevail around the topic of hypnosis and in order to reduce any fears or anxieties which may hold someone back from using this highly effective tool there is a section in this chapter which deals with the most common of these fallacies. When I am asked if hypnosis is 100% effective I will say no and then explain that I believe that the outcome of hypnosis is dependent on a meeting of two minds. The skill of the hypnotist is important for sure. I think that the secret to an effective hypnosis session from what is within the realm of the hypnotherapist is dependant on a number of factors, including listening acutely to what your client or patient is saying and choosing the correct induction and suggestions. There are other factors but that is a whole other book in its own right.

Hypnosis is an interactive therapy so the client must provide correct and honest information. Then, what is often overlooked is the element of expectation and conditioning. Several research studies have found that ones expectation will influence the physiological response to treatment. Did you know that if someone is given an active treatment e.g. a pharmacological drug, and is later given a placebo, the effect of the placebo will be increased? The person sees and feels first hand how effective the drug is and so when they receive a placebo which looks exactly like the drug they expect it to have the same effect and it does indeed have a significant analgesic effect[38]. Other researchers[5] with an interest in this area more recently wanted to know more about how conditioning and cognitive mechanisms influence the placebo response. In essence, from their study with Parkinsons patients and healthy volunteers, they discovered that the physiological processes which we are aware of e.g. pain and motor performance are affected by positive verbal instructions which increase a patients expectations. Furthermore the processes which we are not aware of but which are happening all the time e.g. hormone secretion are not affected by expectation but they are affected by conditioning. This goes back to where the doctor for example administers an active drug, tells the patient they will do well and then that active drug is replaced with a placebo but the patient does not know it is a placebo. Nevertheless, the placebo is effective because the patient has learned to associate taking this tablet with an improvement in health and there is a corresponding effect on the hormones even though this new tablet is medically inactive.

(iv)   Expectation and conditioning

We all adopt patterns of behaviour. It saves time and indeed, brain space. Some psychologists believe that many of these patterns are acquired by means of conditioning. That conditioning can be instrumental or classical. Most of the time behavioural patterns are useful short cuts, for example we may opt for much the same breakfast each day and give it very little thought. This saves time and energy. Repetition of a pattern also means we don't have to re-learn the process each time we want to carry it out so we don't have to think about all the steps involved in brewing our favourite cup of coffee. Habitual behaviour can also develop as a result of chronic pain. We may learn that it is useful to always carry abortive medication just in case the first signs of a migraine arise and so before leaving the house we make sure we have some tablets with us. We may learn to avoid certain activities that aggravate the migraines or we can learn to accept the disability that accompanies migraines and simply resign ourselves to 'putting up with it'. The adage, 'use it or lose it' can be applied to many situations and chronic pain falls comfortably into this raggle-taggle mixture. If we face repeated failure following subsequent attempts to complete a behaviour, for example having the energy to fulfill an eight hour uninterrupted work day, we learn to reduce the working hours to match our energy levels. Another school of thought would advise looking at the factors which affect the energy levels and seeking solutions to rectify those so that the desire to work eight hours and still have lots of energy left over can be accomplished.

You may already be familiar with the Russian physiologist, Pavlov, his dogs and the concept of classical conditioning. Pavlov found that when he presented his dogs with food they started to salivate. He then decided to ring a bell every time food was presented to the dogs. He noticed that the dogs started to salivate every time the bell rang. The dogs had associated the ringing of the bell with the presentation of food and the sound of the bell alone was sufficient to evoke the physiological response of salivation.

Skinner is associated with another form of conditioning, referred to as operant conditioning or instrumental conditioning. This type of learning is based on the fact that behaviour is modified by consequences. It is the carrot and stick system where punishment can be used as a deterrant for unwanted behaviour and praise can be useful for reinforcing a behaviour.

In the example of Pavlov and his dogs a neutral signal such as a bell can be associated with something which was previously neutral so that the neutral response becomes a conditioned stimulus e.g. salivation. All of these processes can occur subtly, beneath our conscious radar. Therefore it would be easy to learn to settle for less and to resign oneself to being powerless over the pain. However, it is also possible to consciously manage the multitude of associations and responses which reflect our day to day living. That way we can govern our response to situations by re-programming our mind to respond in a way which is more beneficial to our lives, our expectations and our needs.

(v) Expect more; break the patterns

So where does this concept of conditioning and expectation fit in with your ProMigraine programme? Well, there is good evidence to support the fact that positive thinking has an affirmative effect on our physiology. Your personal ProMigraine Programme may involve a combination of factors to effectively manage or indeed end your migraines. For some people it will involve lifestyle changes such as more sleep. For another person more sleep combined with hypnosis or meditation might be the best solution. Others could find relief from changing the foods they are eating.

Your body will learn at a conscious level (expectation) that when you follow this plan you will succeed. At a subconscious level (automatic responses) there is good reason to believe that following repeated conditioning, associations will develop so that as you implement your ProMigraine Programme more and more your body will adapt to the changes and the physiological and behavioural changes which you have clearly envisioned will develop.

When you are driving and you come to a red light you do not need to think very long about what that red light requires of you, the driver. Once you have learned that red means stop you will automatically stop at that red light. These subconscious associations are important. They free up our conscious minds to learn more and to observe more. However, when we go to a country where they drive on the opposite side of the road, more of our attention is required initially to adjust to the spatial changes and to over-ride the reflexes. Changing how you manage your migraines will require some effort at first. In time, once you implement the changes which work effectively for you, they will become automatic and results will begin to manifest.

(vi)   Decreasing and eliminating pain with hypnosis

It is worth noting that negative expectations have been shown to induce a decrease in pain tolerance or hyperalgesia (increased sensitivity to pain) in the same way that positive expectations lead to a greater analgesic effect. The lesson here is to think positively and expect great results! If you do it will pay great dividends especially when it comes to pain relief. Hypnosis is proven as an effective treatment for migraines. In fact, a recent review[3] of research studies on this very topic describes hypnosis as a cost effective, non-addictive, rapid and safe alternative to medication in the treatment of migraines. One of the studies[2] described in the review compared a hypnotic intervention using six hypnosis sessions with a group of 23 people and a medication treatment protocol with a group of 24 people. One year after the study the researchers followed up on the participants and found that 10 of the 23 people in the hypnosis group had achieved complete remission from migraines and only 3 of the 24 people in the medication group had achieved the same. Another review[35] a few years prior to this found evidence that hypnotic analgesia is more effective than physical therapy and education/advice in a chronic pain population. If you still have questions about hypnosis I have included information in the next section to help navigate your way around the common misconceptions which shroud hypnosis.

(vii)   Misconceptions of hypnosis debunked

In a hypnosis session there is a common belief that the client will be under the control of a domineering hypnotist, that they will reveal all their deeply buried secrets and that they will not hear a thing. The incorrect perception is understandable. Multiple misconceptions about hypnosis shroud this intervention in clouds of fear. Sweeping statements espoused by those with little specialist knowledge on the topic have, inadvertently perhaps, weaved a web of mystery around a physiologically and psychologically sound process which can facilitate rapid change.

The association of hypnosis with sleep may be an understandable observation given that individuals in a state of hypnosis during demonstrations and in clinic situations usually have their eyes closed. It is an obvious deduction to make unless otherwise informed. In reality the time before sleep is actually very similar to the trance state but the brain waves are different when one falls into the state of sleep itself. It is the daydreaming type of state, the 'aware but not aware' feeling of detachment which is more correctly characteristic of hypnosis. For the person in hypnosis this means that they will hear everything they choose to focus upon and if they choose to focus their attention inwardly on another thought or outwardly on a noise or other distractions it is their choice. Most of the time they will still be aware that the hypnotist is speaking but may not hear what they are saying. This happens normally in everyday life also. If you have ever been pre-occupied with something and, try as you might to maintain an interest in an ongoing conversation, the mind wanders and the words of those in your company may as well be floating over your head for all that you hear. Prolonged lectures on a topic of little interest can potentially have the same effect.. Somehow, in this hypnotic state however, if suggestions are relevant, they have an impact on our thought processes and our subsequent behaviour.

The persuasive and devious Svengali archetypal figure still associated with hypnosis to the present day has served a purpose to some extent. It adds mystery and mysique to the area of hypnosis and given the gaps in our knowledge about the physiological underpinnings of the hypnotic process it is no surprise such aspirations thrive. One of the greatest fears people report when the topic of hypnosis arises is the fear that they will reveal something that they do not wish to share. The fact is that you are in control while in a state of hypnosis. If it is a suggestion work type of session, which typically, weight loss and smoking tend to be then you will not need to say a single word while you are in the hypnotic trance. There is another part to hypnosis, referred to as regression work or analytical work. This involves trawling back through memories to discover the reasons for a current pattern of behaviour that the person wishes to change. It may be used for the treatment of Bruxism (grinding teeth at night), panic attacks and nail biting for example. Nevertheless, you will always be in control of what you choose to say and what you choose not to say. In fact, you will be so in control that you will be able to open your eyes and walk out of the door of the hypnotists office any time you choose to.

Another popular misconception about hypnosis is that you will be completely unaware of everything; unable to hear what the hypnotist is saying. All senses are heightened in hypnosis so the reverse is true. When you think about it rationally, if you have ever watched a stage hypnotist persuade his participants to forget their telephone numbers or imagine they are Superman/Wonderwoman as the case may be, the participants will need to hear everything that is being said in order to respond then it makes sense.

A common belief about hypnosis regards the perception of the hypnotized persons intelligence. Without exploring into the physiological differences which delineate those who are highly hypnotizable from those who are moderately hypnotizable at this point in time, it may be of interest to note that those who enter the state of hypnosis easily usually have excellent attentional ability ~ an asset rather than a curse when it comes to learning and memory.

So, rest assured that the hypnotic experience is an interactional one where you hear everything, you remain in control of what you say and how you choose to respond. Those who respond well are usually focused individuals with good attentional ability and a good hypnotist will adapt their style, be it passive or authorative to the requirements of their client.

(viii) What to expect from a hypnotherapist dealing with migraines

If you decide to visit an hypnotherapist about your migraines they will probably ask you about the frequency and duration of those migraines. It would be useful if they recorded the severity of your migraines before and after the work you do together also. If you have an idea of when your migraines are most likely to occur and the triggers which seem to cause your migraines this information will be very useful for your hypnotherapist. Remember too to mention any activities which you find difficult to commit to or anything which you have given up because of your migraines. The hypnotherapist will then guide you in to a state of trance. You will be able to hear everything that they are saying although many people find that they drift away into their own thoughts during a session. A typical, straight forward, suggestion-type hypnosis session will generally last approximately one hour and for about thirty to forty minutes you will be in trance. The number of sessions required for long-term relief from migraines will vary from person to person but you should notice an improvement even after the first session. It is a very pleasant experience and a state which you will be familiar with as we go in and out of trance every day. Have you ever been on a long bus journey and even though you are looking out the window, if you were asked what you had seen, it would be difficult to remember? The probability is high that you were in a trance like state. If someone had called your name or if your attention was required for any reason you would have come straight out of the trance with ease and you would have responded to the person who had requested your attention. The results you achieve will be dependent on the hypnotherapist having a thorough understanding of hypnosis and migraines and the information which you volunteer to them during your consultation. You will be perfectly aware leaving the office and very often it is only with hindsight that you may notice the difference. Typical comments on session two are 'I didn't even think about my migraines and I got so much work done,' or 'It was only when I came back to work on Monday that I realised it was probably the first weekend in a long time when I didn't have to go to bed for a few hours during the day.'

(ix)   The ProMigraine hypnosis programme

The ProMigraine Hypnosis Programme addresses a number of areas typically affecting migraine sufferers. It can be downloaded from the internet in just a few minutes and it can be a very useful package for anyone diagnosed with migraine. The programme itself was developed as part of a PhD programme. After working for ten years as a hypnotherapist the tacit knowledge gleaned through working with so many people - many of whom had migraines - has contributed enormously to building this product. There are six mp3s for you to download with or without the book. Each mp3 is focused on a significant area related to migraines. One of the mp3s for example is designed to decrease the physical pain of migraine. Another is designed to help the user regain a feeling of control over a part of their life which may have seemed out of control. The series also contains an mp3 which uses a beautiful metaphor of a picturesque castle to erase past thought processes which may have caused or contributed to migraines. The variety of mp3s in the pack means you will be able to focus on a specific part of migraines that bothers you most or you could choose to listen to all of them and target different disabilities caused by migraine. Whether you decide to use hypnosis as part of your programme or not, the website www.promigraine.com can keep you informed on up-to-date information about migraines and there is a free general relaxation mp3 which you can download from the website too, and like the ProMigraine Programme, you can listen to it at a time that suits you.

Choice Management

"Character is that which reveals moral purpose, exposing the class of things a man chooses and avoids."

Aristotle

(i)   Decision making

Go for a run or don't go for a run.....watch television or listen to the radio...study or relax....low fat or full fat...Every day we face a myriad of choices from the moment we wake up in the morning. The heuristics and patterns of behaviour which we create allow us to function largely at a subconscious level. We don't really need to think about how to make a cup of coffee for example. It is an automatic process. Most of us will eat more or less the same thing for breakfast every morning. These patterns require little brain space and very little of our attention. If you currently have a routine for managing your migraines and it works for you as you want it to, it probably places very little demand on your time. For those who are happy with taking medication for example, it certainly is effective for many people who have migraines and can be a very fast solution to pain. It can also have side effects however and medication can be expensive. If you are unhappy with the severity and frequency of your migraines then you need to weigh up your options. Choosing to instigate a new management plan will take up more of your time. Thus you need to weigh up the cost and the benefit. It might save you more money in the long term or, it might cost you more. It might decrease your migraines to a fraction of the number you used to suffer but it may require that you are more mindful of what you eat or it may demand that you set aside twenty minutes of each day to meditate. What type of time and financial commitment you invest and whether the investment pays sufficient dividends is dependent on your priorities as an individual and your own personal belief system and goals.

(ii)   A valuable investment

Chances are, if you have ever played a sport or learned to play music, the first time you played your skills would have been unsophisticated and raw. Then as you practised you learned how to execute a piece of music or a sports move with greater dexterity. After more rehearsal it may be that you became so accomplished that you no longer even had to think about it. If you decide to investigate and follow the ProMigraine Programme there is no getting away from the initial investment in time and attention which will be required. The first requirement for learning a new pattern of thinking and behaviour is conscious attention. There might well be a few frustrating moments as you discover some aspects of the plan, which simply do not fit in with your lifestyle. There may well be other moments along the way which are peppered with split second insights, opening the mind to opportunities which can contribute to a life with fewer migraines. As Socrates said, 'wisdom begins in wonder'.

In the next few paragraphs we will explore why and how the initial, additional pain of concentration, research and rehearsal can pay huge dividends for migraine sufferers.

The first step towards
accomplishment of your goals is:

Attention, Attention, Attention

(iii)   *Information processing*

A basic overview of information processing may help to explain how even the most complex of tasks can become automatic with the correct application. Information processing involves the structure of how we process what we see, hear and feel in the world around us and what happens to that information once we pay attention to it. Imagine, for example, that you have taken up basketball and on one of your fourth or fifth practice session your coach decides to demonstrate a specific drill such as dribbling. You will run through a number of processes in your mind - all of which are invisible to the observer. First the mind interprets that you need to translate the words being spoken into a command to move your eyes in the direction of the person who is demonstrating the new drill. Then you will narrow your attention to the coach's actions whether that means looking at the way their hands are dribbling the ball or the way their feet are moving. Thirdly you will have an expectation from what you have learned already in the previous practice sessions of what can be done with the basketball. Life is never that simple however and it can happen that, while you are trying to internalise all of this information, a team-mate yells at you from the side of the court. Your attention is distracted momentarily and you disengage from watching the coach who is demonstrating the task. When the coach suddenly lets go of the basketball, your attention re-engages and follows the basketball as it bounces down the court... There is a lot happening in the brain!

(iv) One step at a time

The important question an aspiring athlete should be asking in this situation is if it is possible to focus on the individual demonstrating the drill, and at the same time block out the background noise and take in as much information about the drill as possible. The answer to the question is yes. If you think back to any great sporting achievements which you watched or participated in, you may remember being completely focused and in a place where you were unaware of anyone being around you. You displayed an ability to ignore external distractions. Attention is an elaborate process. The relatively recent advent of fMRI and PET scans which can give a visual image of activity in the brain have demonstrated how several areas of the brain appear to be involved in cognitive tasks which involve attention[52]. As you gain a greater understanding of attention and information processing, you will see how you can use this knowledge to your advantage in any area of your life, including managing the pain of migraines. There is a considerable amount of information to think about initially when devising your ProMigraine Programme so it can be helpful to consider it in stages, one step at a time.

(v) Repetition, information processing and migraines

Once you weigh up your options and affirm the goals which you have for your ProMigraine Programme, and assess how much time you are willing to invest to achieve those goals, you can then explore a variety of options. You can rule out options which do not work for you and discover the ones which are effective and which fit in with your lifestyle. Following the preliminary elimination process, one chronic migraine sufferer may find for example that investing fifteen minutes, four times a week listening to a hypnosis recording will cut the number of migraine hours from 43 hours a week to 8 hours a week. If they were confined to bed for days with their migraines, their small investment of an hour each week is ultimately giving them back a day and a half of their life every single week. Each week or month it might be useful to draw up a SWOT analysis to evaluate how effective each particular plan is for you. Just like any other learned skill in life, once you get used to the ProMigraine

Programme that works for you, you will notice that you need to think about it less and less. It will essentially become part of your everyday lifestyle. After a while you will become so adept that even when life throws the occasional curveball in your direction you can bounce back quickly and easily.

When you formulate the best plan of action:

Repeat, Repeat, Repeat,

(vi)   *When patterns become automatic*

When you practice a skill over and over again the brain sets in motion a connection of neurons that have a weak connection at first. Then, with repetition, they become stronger. Once the neural pattern is established it is a little bit like dominos in some respects. When you push the first domino the rest follow. If you set them up the way you want them to fall then you achieve the desired result. To revert to the sporting analogy, it is important therefore to have a good coach from the outset and to learn the skill properly from the beginning. For any pain management programme it is essential that you read sufficient relevant material. The more you practice a specific drill, the stronger the neural connections become. Eventually very little conscious attention is required and the pattern becomes faster. The response is therefore faster and there is an automaticity to the process so you barely have to think about what to do. This then frees up more attentional processing space in the brain so you can take in more information around you in the environment. In practical terms this means you have more brain space available to see what is happening around you at any given moment in time. This should then lead to a faster response time. The analogy most frequently used in the literature to explain this process is that of driving a car. Initially when we learn to drive we are looking to see where the clutch is, the brake, the accelerator. So much brain space is taken up with co-ordinating the clutch and accelerator and brake that there are less resources to pay attention to what is actually happening on the road. As you practice, driving becomes automatic, the neural patterns are hardwired and moved down to a different part of the brain so you don't even seem to pay attention to the mechanics of driving. This leaves more brain space available for looking at the road and paying attention to what is happening around you. Taking time out to analyse the contributory factors which trigger your migraines and assessing the various options available to minimise the number, frequency and intensity of your migraines requires more attentional resources in the initial stages. However, once a solution is found that helps you to achieve your goals, the process becomes easier, less time consuming, and eventually will reach the point where you hardly need to devote any attention to it at all.

(vii)   Repetition, Repetition, Repetition

It is the migraine equivalent for the Estate Agent's mantra 'Location, Location, Location'. Same too for music as Philip Ball explains in his book 'The Music Instinct'. In his research on musicians and the cognitive map which resides in their heads Ball cites a study about young student musicians who were rated by their professors. Those who rated high in the estimation of the professors were found to have put in 10,000 hours of practice as compared to the 5,000 hours practice clocked up by their less talented classmates. To understand what is happening in the brain when you commit a skill or a pattern of behaviour to memory, it can help to know a little about Long Term Potentiation (LTP) and neurons. There are billions of neurons in each human brain and between each neuron is a synapse. Neurotransmitters, some of which you may be familiar with such as dopamine and serotonin are released into the synapses on a constant basis. LTP is a course of action across neurons in the brain. It is important for learning and memory[17]. When you experience anything, neuronal firing occurs and the action of LTP can make it easier for subsequent information to fire along the same neuronal pathway. When the experience is repeated, the message becomes more permanent and this is facilitated by LTP which enhances synaptic transmission. LTP facilitates stronger connections between neurons by either increasing the number of post-synaptic receptors or by making the existing post-synaptic receptors more sensitive[47]. More and more neurons are recruited and the web of neurons becomes stronger and is then moved to memory. When you find a plan that works for you and serves to minimise the number and severity of your migraines, stick to it. Then, when life throws an unexpected twist or turn you can rise to the challenge and adapt your plan with ease.

(viii) Adapting to new challenges

It may be that from time to time you need to reassess your ProMigraine Programme. Life moves on, we meet new challenges and new people. There might be more stress or less stress. The body and mind need to be challenged in order to progress. If you feel migraines are affecting your life in an extremely adverse way, it might be worth it to keep track of the number of migraines you have each week and month, the plan you are followed that week, whether there were any exceptionally stressful situations that month and so on. Retrospectively, after a year, you should have a pretty good idea of the patterns which helped and which hindered your migraine plan.

Some people will uncover what works for them very quickly and for others it may well involve a process of elimination until the migraine management goals are achieved. One person, for example, might find that eliminating cheese and chocolate and going for a walk each evening to reduce stress levels works for them. After a while, with repetition, the pattern becomes as natural as breathing.

(ix) Being alert to helpful signposts

We all have schemata, that is, mental representations which organise our assumptions and the information we have about something. Schemata will influence our attention, for example if you decide to buy a new car in the morning, let's take the example of a new Ford Focus, you are likely to notice many more of the same model car on the road over the following weeks. It is not that others have decided to change their car for a Ford Focus as well, it is simply that it is in our consciousness and we tend to notice things which ally with our schemata. In terms of migraines and managing migraines, you are likely to find that you become very adept for example, at picking out choices on a menu which will not trigger a migraine. Another example might be sitting down to plan your day and finding that, because you have prioritised your Promigraine Programme goals there is plenty of time each day to relax or to fit in the appointments which support you in achieving your goals.

Attitude

"The one thing you can't take away from me is the way I choose to respond to what you do to me. The last of one's freedoms is to choose ones attitude in any given circumstance."

Victor Frankl

(i)   The importance of attitude

Attitude. It constitutes the final chapter of the book, but it may well be the most important chapter. Attitude embodies our thinking and behaviour. I believe it also reflects our soul. It is reflected in the very way we regard a situation, person or thing. Viktor Frankl, author of 'Man's Search For Meaning' observed the commonalities and differences among those who shared his experience in a concentration camp.

Frankl understood the impact of attitude and the need for purpose. He notes in his book that those who survived had, in their minds eye, a reason to live and he frequently quotes from Frederich Nietzche; "He who has a why to live for can bear almost any how". Frankl survived the Holocaust but his observations from the concentration camp continued to shape his life thereafter. He mused that we all need to find meaning in our lives. That meaning, he suggests, may be the love for another person, achieving something poignant in work or the demonstration of courage in times of hardship. It is difficult to disagree. Everyone needs a purpose in life. When we have purpose, we have a reason to survive. When that purpose is lost, hope is destroyed.

(ii)   Attitude and health

It is human nature to take good health for granted when we have not experienced the alternate. When disease or illness take hold, it is usually only then that we realise the great gifts that we had all along. Those gifts include energy, freedom and time. Migraine may not be the most debilitating of the neurological disorders but it is certainly disruptive. In their worst, most chronic form, migraines have the capacity to rob one of copious amounts of time and put a sudden halt to activities which for most people are routine jobs such as shopping or working. Migraines can have a mischievous effect on our mental health too. The uncertainty as to when they will strike can cause fearful thoughts and mental barriers to what we can and cannot potentially plan for. Migraines can disrupt holidays, upset work schedules and leave their unhappy victims in a permanent state of uncertainty – if ill-managed. Thus a positive attitude coupled with a personal action plan can thankfully alleviate most of these problems.

(iii)   Establishing your meaning and purpose

I practised as a sport psychologist for many years and during that time it was an honour to work with both amateur and professional athletes. Their drive to win was divided into two camps: those who wanted to continue to beat their own personal goals time and time again and those who wanted to surpass the achievements of others. It seemed to me that the former was the individual with a healthier attitude and the more achievable goals. Environments are different from person to person. Circumstances are different too. While I do not dispute the fact that it is beneficial to look towards others for inspiration and in fact model some of the behaviour of those who inspire us, I believe that each person has their own solutions and their own answers. Given the courage and insight to listen to those beliefs, accept why we want to achieve those goals and subsequently follow those convictions a road map to achieving those goals can then be created.

You may recall in chapter one of your workbook you were called upon to paint a picture of all of the things you could do if migraines were a less prevalent part of your life or indeed if they were no longer a part of your life. Now is time to revisit that plan and make a note of how you would *feel* on an emotional level if you could fill your life with all the plans, activities and goals for the present and the future if migraines no longer had a hold on your day to day routine. Once the meaning and purpose are established then there may well be no better time than the present to take action and pursue that plan which you feel is most appropriate for your personal beliefs and circumstances.

Conclusion

Environment - inside and out, impacts the experience of migraine. If you are vulnerable to migraine, there are a number of variables which precipitate and can subsequently aggravate migraines. The objective of this book, along with the workbook, is to help you to identify the migraine provoking factors which are specific to you and provide some reasons for and encouragement to make changes within these areas. We all have a limited amount of time on this earth. For most of us, how that time is viewed, how that time is used and the people chosen to share that time with, really is within our control. The nascent investment of time spent diagnosing migraine triggers, aggravators and alleviators, admittedly is demanding. For some, medication will be effective and will save time. However, the long-term potential pay-off in terms of time saved instead of spent on suffering with migraine, coupled with the economic, psychological and social rewards can yield equal or greater dividends worth considering for those who wish to pursue the alternate road. The choice is always yours. I wish you well along your journey to great health.

Workbook

PART I

The Facts

Data Collection:

Looking back:

- In the past month, how many hours and days were stolen from you because of migraine?
- In the past month, how many migraines did you suffer?
- In the past month, how severe on a scale of 1 to 5 were your migraines; 1 being mild and 5 being very severe.
- List all of the activities and events which you could not start or complete because of migraines.

Looking forward:

- How badly do you want to manage or eliminate migraines form your life?
- What are you willing to do in order to manage your migraines?
- How much time are you willing to set aside each week to create a migraine management programme to help you to decrease the severity, duration and frequency of your migraines?
- What benefits have you noticed as a result of having migraines?
- What would your life be like without migraines?

Define Your Migraine:

Do you suffer from
- a) Common migraine
- b) Classic migraine

What stages of migraine do you generally experience?
- a) Prodrome
- b) Aura
- c) Migraine
- d) Restorative
- e) Postdrome

How many hours did you lose this month because of migraines?

_____

What did you have to stop because of migraines interrupting your life?

Work   _____
Social life   _____
Family time   _____
Other   _____

Were you happy to have an excuse not to do any of these things?

What events, situations and experiences were you disappointed to have missed out on, because of migraines, this month?

Work Migraine Balance:

This month record the frequency and duration of your migraines in the table below. See example in row one. Then after one month add up the total number of hours in column three and write it in to column four.

Date	Day	Duration of migraine	Total hours this month
12 August 2012	Sunday	10 hours	

Financial Burdens:

Migraines cost money - both for the individual who suffers with them and also society. How much money are you losing personally from absenteeism or disability?

If you have not considered this before, please use the chart below and on the next page to monitor the number of days you are losing to migraines each month and the earnings you could potentially make if you had the capacity to work on these days.

Date of absenteeism from work due to Migraine	Potential or real Income Lost $/€	Date of absenteeism from work due to Migraine	Potential or real Income Lost $/€
Total Cost per annum $/€			

	Total no. of days per month	Total Cost per month
Jan		
Feb		
March		
April		
May		
June		
July		
August		
September		
October		
November		
December		

Add up the total cost per annum and make a list below of what you would use this money for had you earned it.

1._____
2._____
3._____

Cost of Medication:

You have already established how much pain and disruption migraines have made in your life. Now it is time to consider the best plan of action going forward.

There is an opportunity cost with every decision you make. If you decide to proceed with the ProMigraine Programme, you first need to do a cost-benefit analysis of medication and if you find that medication is not helping you manage your migraines as well as you would like, then it may be time to consider an alternate migraine management plan such as the ProMigraine Programme.

Fill in the chart below for a period of three months prospectively or retrospectively.

Month/Year				
Total Medication in mg taken this month				
Total cost of medication each month €/$				
Total cost of GP/Neurologist/Pain Specialist appointments each month				
Rough estimate of how effective you estimate the medication to be on a 0 to10 scale Where 0= not at all effective 10= eliminates migraines				

Part II

Eliminating Triggers

Quick Checklist:

Please tick any of the following that you are aware of which trigger your migraine:

Nutrition	
Sleep	
Holidays/Travel	
Exercise	
Psychological Stress	
Injury to head or neck	
Medication	
Weather	
Physical Exertion	
Hormonal fluctuations	
Fasting	
Bright Lights/Strong Smells, Loud Noise	

Environment:

Which environmental factors have acted as a trigger for your migraines in the past?

- Weather: Humidity/Heat/Other.. (please indicate) _____
- Air Pollution: _____
- Noise _____
- Bright lights_____
- Smells (please be specific e.g. certain perfumes)_____
- Computer Screen_____
- Posture_____
- Other (please be specific)_____

Write those you have highlighted in the box below and in the column to the right of each one, enter a potential solution, if any, that you can think of. See line one for an example.

Environmental Triggers	Potential Solution
Example: Computer Screen Posture	Adjust flicker Use an ergonomically designed chair

Perception, Thoughts, Behaviour and Physiology:

Environment plays a significant role on how we feel emotionally. Subsequently this will reflect on our physiology.

Where do you spend most of your time? You can average it out over a week and write the numbers in the furthermost column. Divide the divisions below into percentage as per the example.

	Example	
Home	30%	
Work	60%	
Social situations	10%	
Other (please specify)		

When you feel a migraine coming on, how much time will you have spent in any of these environments for the preceding 24 hours.

	Example	
Home	90%	
Work		
Social situations	10%	
Other (please specify)		

In the example above, the migraine patient explained that most of their migraines occur on a Sunday when they generally will have spent the previous day relaxing at home after an arduous week of work.

These forms are not designed to discover any contributory factors of your migraines. Their purpose is solely to highlight areas you need to be more conscious of as to when a migraine attack might occur. In that way you can be prepared to take action with your own personal migraine management action plan.

Social Setting:

Once you have your own personal ProMigraine management plan how will it impact your life, your social network of friends and family, your time, your work, your recreational activities? Paint the picture of the life you envision for yourself in words which mean something to you.

_____

_____

_____

Describe in three sentences how you wish your life to be, for example, do you expect to be reduce or eliminate migraines from your life and what will you do with the time which used to be commandeered and restricted by the pain of migraine.

_____

_____

_____

Restoring Balance:

1. How much do you believe that you will find a way to manage your migraines effectively on a scale of 0 to 10? Please circle.

0   1   2   3   4   5   6   7   8   9   10

No belief   Somewhat believe   Absolutely 100% believe

2. What change in your life would prove to you that you are making progress in managing your migraines?

3. Small steps: How can you make initial progress with your migraine management plan? What is the first step which would show you that your plan is going to be effective in delivering what you desire from your migraine management plan?

How much time are you willing to invest in discovering and creating a plan which will work for you to restore optimal good health? 2 hours a month, a week or a day for the first two, three, or four months, weeks or days?

Nutrition:

Which of the following did you have preceding a migraine attack? Fill in the columns over a few weeks/months and notice any patterns which emerge. See column one for an example. In the blank boxes add any which are relevant but not listed.

Date	Example 08/08/12					
Red Wine	✓					
Cheese						
Chocolate	✓					
Fasting						
Citrus Fruits						
Ice-Cream						
Herring						
Chicken						
High Fat Diet						

Supplements and Fat Grams:

Do you take any supplements e.g. feverfew or magnesium and have you found them to be beneficial?

Supplements   *Efficacy:* (please write helpful or not helpful beside supplement)

1. Feverfew   _____
2. Magnesium   _____
3. Other (please list)   _____

Calorie and Fat Counting:

How many calories do you eat on a daily basis?
How many grams of fat do you eat on a daily basis? _____g
Choose a typical day and keep a food diary in the table below, recording the total number of calories and total number of fat grams per day.

Food	Calories	Grams of fat in this serving
Total		

If you find that there are indications that you are eating a high fat diet it may be advisable to contact a nutritionist to help you change your eating plan.

Stress Manager:

First we will create a snapshot of your life in general. Then we will look at the triggers which contribute to your migraines in general.

Identifying stressors:

Identify and categorise various areas of your life as shown in the illustration example on the next page. You can add more categories and change the names of each category. Then draw a line, roughly representing how much stress you feel in relation to each category on average, on a daily basis. Closer to the left indicates less stress and closer to the right indicates more stress. In this example on the next page the person has indicated that they have quite high stress levels around the area of finances and reasonably low levels of stress in relation to family and home life.

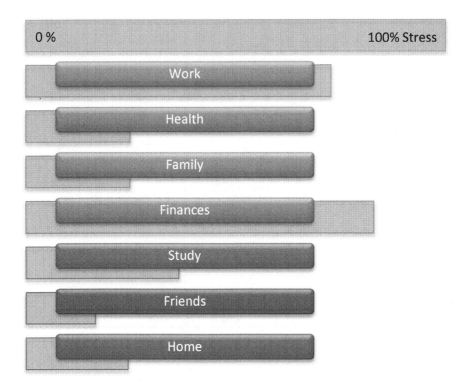

| 0 % | 100% Stress |

Work

Health

Family

Finances

Study

Friends

Home

Your turn:

In the drawing on the next page:
  a) Write down the various categories around which your life congregates similar to the example above.

  b) Draw a line representing the level of stress for each category.

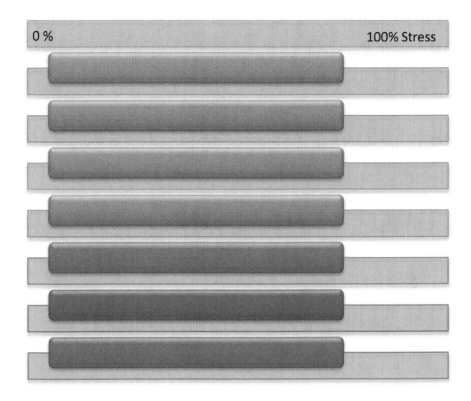

0 %   100% Stress

Identifying other Migraine Triggers:

Do the same with the factors which you have identified as triggering your migraines in the past. Follow the example on page 116. In this example the person has indicated that any sudden changes in their lifestyle, such as an abrupt change from a pattern of high activity at work to a relaxing weekend is very likely to be followed by a migraine attack. Travel is also highly likely to trigger an attack. In this example foods occasionally trigger a migraine attack but this individual has identified and avoids the foods in question and so food is no longer likely to precipitate an attack. Heat, Stress, Strong Smells and Loud Sounds do not currently lead to a migraine attack in this person.

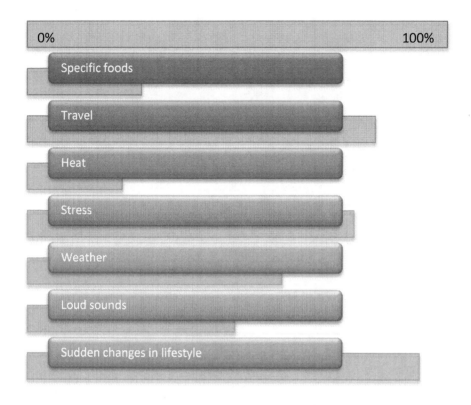

0%   100%

- Specific foods
- Travel
- Heat
- Stress
- Weather
- Loud sounds
- Sudden changes in lifestyle

Your turn:

a) In the table on page 117 make a list of any and all triggers which currently or in the past have precipitated a migraine attack.

b) Draw a line to indicate the potency of these migraine precipitators in your life <u>at this point in time.</u>

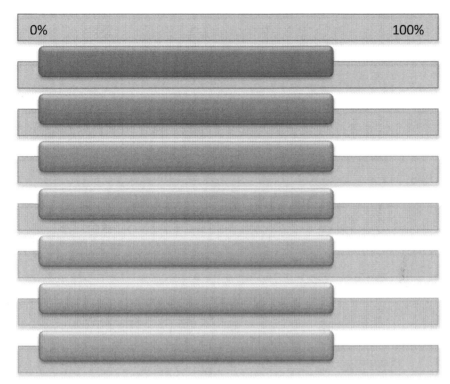

Instigating change to reduce stress:

What needs to change in your life to reduce your stress levels? Using the information from both diagrams, make a list of those events and situations and migraine triggers which you have highlighted that contribute to your migraines. Start with the event or trigger which causes you the most stress and write down what you are going to do to reduce those stress levels. See the examples below.

Event	Stress Level %	Action for change	Time Frame

Sudden Change in lifestyle 90% Wind down from work gradually not abruptly start today
Travel   80%   Listen to meditation cds prior to and during flights
Finance   70%   Seek advice of career guidance counsellor by August 8th

Sleep:

Do you ever have problems initiating sleep i.e. getting to sleep?

Do you have problems maintaining sleep i.e. staying asleep?

Do you ever experience any of the following? Please tick any which are applicable.

- Restless leg syndrome_____

- Snoring_____

- Sleep apnea (when breathing becomes very shallow and it brings you out of deep sleep) ___

- Awakening headaches (where a headache wakes you up from sleep) _____

Over the next month please record the number of hours you sleep and the incidence of migraine.

Date	Hours Sleep	Migraine yes/no

Part III

Factors Influencing Your Success

Natural Remedies for Migraine:

Monitoring the efficacy of natural supplements and treatments:

With the advice of your health care professional, if you decide to use any of the novel supplements such as Riboflavin, Magnesium or Feverfew or treatments such as Osteopathy or Physiotherapy, it can be useful to make a note of your experience with them.

Date	Alternate Treatment	Effect
Example: *1st June 2012 to 1st August 2012*	*Example:* Magnesium 400mg supplement	*Example:* Had fewer migraines over the past two months. Have also used meditation cds. No side effects noticed.

Exercise:

On page 122 you will find a table where you can conduct your own personal research into how exercise affects your migraine. The Borg Scale is a Ratings of Perceived Exertion Scale which correlates with VO_{2max} and is very easy to use. It can give you a good idea of the intensity of your workout and then, after a few months you can compare it to your migraine frequency, severity and intensity chart and see if there are any overlaps which would indicate any possible changes which occurred as a result of your exercise regime. See the table on page 121 for a suggested indicator which could be used to rate the severity of your migraine.

Severity of Migraine Indicator

A	B	C	D
Mild	Moderate	Severe	Unbearable

About the Borg Scale of Perceived Exertion

When using the Borg scale to judge the intensity of your workload while exercising bear in mind that a rating of 6 on a scale of 6 to 20 would represent a level of activity where you are at rest and feeling very relaxed. A self-rating of 11 might be the equivalent of someone ambling at a comfortable pace. A self-rating of 13 would be indicative of an activity or pace which is challenging while a self-rating of 15 to 17 would represent a hard to very hard level of activity. If you were to rate your intensity at 20 this would indicate a level of intensity which is an absolute maximum and would be unsustainable for a lengthy period of time.

Training Tracker:

Date	Exercise Type	Borg Scale intensity	Migraine yes/no Duration in hours Severity A-D
Example: 23 October 2012	Running	16	No migraine today

Time Management:

List the priorities in your life:
1.
2.
3.
4.
5.
6.
7.
8.

How is your time currently allocated on a typical day?

Time am/pm	Activity	No. of Hours
_____	_____	_____
_____	_____	_____
_____	_____	_____
_____	_____	_____
_____	_____	_____
_____	_____	_____
_____	_____	_____
_____	_____	_____
_____	_____	_____

Cost Benefit Analysis:

What is this *current* plan of action costing you?

    a) emotionally:

    b) physically:

    c) spiritually:

What are your strengths?
Example: great time keeper

What are your weaknesses?

If you were to adopt a new plan of action which capitalised on your strengths and allowed you to outsource the things you find difficult or too time consuming what would your life be like?

How would this *new* plan of action affect you?

    a) emotionally:

    b) physically:

    c) spiritually:

Changing Times:

How can you allocate your time better and still meet the priorities in your life?

Time am/pm	Activity	No. of Hours
_____	_____	_____
_____	_____	_____
_____	_____	_____
_____	_____	_____
_____	_____	_____
_____	_____	_____

Hypnosis, words and migraines:

What words and phrases do you use when you speak or think about your migraines? If you are not aware of them right now monitor how you refer to your migraines and write down those words over the next month. You may be surprised at the significance words have and the impact they have on you.

Words:

Phrases:

Is there a better way to reframe these words and phrases? Use the space below to alter those thought patterns.

Remember, words, whether spoken aloud or held in our thoughts have an impact on our physiology. You have the power to change those words and phrases and thus alter your physiology.

If you have never used hypnosis what are the reasons for this?

Write your reason in the box on the left. Then see if you can figure out a potential solution.

Reason	Potential Solution
Example: Fear of hypnosis	Read the section on misconceptions about hypnosis in this book

Choice Management:

What outcome would you like to have from your ProMigraine Management Plan? (*e.g. reduce the severity of migraines from level D to a A, or reduce the number of migraines from one a week to one a month*).

_____

_____

_____

How much time do you <u>currently</u> set aside each week to <u>manage</u> your migraines (*e.g. 5 minutes to take some prophylactic medication with a view to stopping it before it starts*).

_____

_____

_____

How much time are you <u>willing</u> to set aside to manage your migraines?

The first month _____

The second month _____

Subsequent months _____

Remember, during the first two months you will be looking at different options to suit you so more time may be required initially. Once a plan is in place and operational something like ninety minutes of yoga or meditation a week might be enough to cut the number of hours previously consumed by migraines in half. That could be regarded as a very good return on ones investment.

Perform a SWOT analysis on each plan as you explore each option: e.g. acupuncture once a week and remove all foods from diet which may aggravate the migraines.

Strengths	Weaknesses
Felt very relaxed after acupuncture. I had fewer migraines and they were nothing near as severe in intensity as they were before starting this plan.	Found it difficult to stay away from the foods which I like but which seem to trigger the migraines
Opportunities	Threats
I will have time at the weekend to write a list of potential substitutes for those foods so that I won't be stuck for choice. I could spend the extra hours that were tied up being in bed with migraine doing some part time work or relaxing.	Acupuncture is expensive so I may not be able to afford to go as often as I need.

Your turn:

Plan for month one:

Strengths	Weaknesses
Opportunities	**Threats**

Attitude:

How will you *feel* when your migraines are less frequent or are completely under control?

What activities will you fill your life with when you have your own personal migraine management system working for you?

What positive emotions will fill your life when you take on the activities or include proper restorative rest times that you desire?

When are you going to take action?

References

1. Aguggia, M., Cavallini, M., Divito, N., Ferrero, M., Lentini, A., Montano, V., et al. (2011). Sleep and primary headaches. *Neurological Sciences*, 32, 51-54.
2. Anderson, J.A., Basker, M.A. & Dalton, R. (1975). Migraine and hypnotherapy. *International Journal of Clinical and Experimental Hypnosis*, 23, 48-58.
3. Ball. P. (2010). *The Music Instinct.* Oxford University Press. USA. Badley head.
4. Benedetti, F. (2007) The Placebo and Nocebo Effect: How the therapists words act on the patient's brain. *Karger Gazette. Mind & Body.* 69, 7-9.
5. Benedetti, F., Pollo, A., Lopiano, L., Lanotte, M., Vighetti, S., & Rainero, I. (2003). Conscious expectation and unconscious conditioning in analgesic, motor and hormonal placebo/nocebo responses. *Journal of Neuroscience.* 23(10), 4315-4323.
6. Benoit, D.P. (2009). An introduction to migraine pathophysiology. *Techniques in Regional Anaesthesia & Pain Management.* 13, 5-8.
7. Bic, Z., Blix, G.G., Hopp, H.P., Leslie, F.M., & Schell, M.J. (1999). The influence of a low-fat diet on the incidence and severity of migraine headaches. *Journal of Women's Health & Gender-Based Medicine.* 8(5), 623-630.

8. Bigal, M.E., Borucho, S., Serrano, D., & Lipton, R.B. The acute treatment of episodic and chronic migraine in the USA. *Cephalagia.* Aug, 29(8), 891-897.

9. Blau, J.N. (1987). *Migraine: Clinical and Research Aspects.* The John Hopkins University Press. Baltimore.

10. Boehnke, C., Reuter, U., Flach, U., Schuh-Hofer, S., Einha¨upl K.L. & Arnold, G. (2004). High-dose riboflavin treatment is efficacious in migraine prophylaxis: an open study in a tertiary care centre. *European Journal of Neurology.* 11, 475-477

11. *Bruce Lipton (2005). The Biology of Belief.* Mountain of Love/ Elite Books. Santa Rosa, CA.

12. Busch, V. & Gaul, C. (2008). Exercise in migraine therapy – Is there any evidence for efficacy? A critical review. *Headache,* 48, 890-899.

13. Calhoun, A.H., Ford, S., Finkel, A.G., Kahn, K.A. & Mann, J.D. (2006). The prevalence and spectrum of sleep problems in women with transformed migraine. *Headache: The Journal of Head & Face Pain.* 46(4), 604-610.

14. Cevoli, S., Giannini, G., Favoni, V., Pierangeli, G., & Cortelli, P. (2012). Migraine and sleep disorders. *Neurological Science.* May; 33, supp1 43-46.

15. Chasman,D.I., Schurks, M., Antilla, V., et al. Genome-wide association study reveals three susceptibility loci for common migraine in the general population. *Nature Genetics.* 43, 695-698.

16. Chen, M., Fan, X., & Moe, S. (2002). Criterion-related validity of the Borg ratings of perceived exertion scale in healthy individuals. Journal of Sports Science. 20(11), 873-879.

17. Cooke S.F. & Bliss, T.V. (2006). Plasticity in the human central nervous system. *Brain.* 129(7), 1659–73.

18. Darabaneanu, S., Overath, C.H., Rubin, D., Lüthje, S., Sye, W., (2011). Aerobic exercise as a therapy option for migraine: a pilot study. *International Journal of Sports Medicine.* 32(6), 455-60.

19. Ducros, A. (2006). Physiopathologie et approche génétique de la migraine. (French). *Mechanisms and Genetics of Migraine. (English), 20,* 1-11.

20. Finocchi, C. & Giorgia, S. (2012). Food as trigger and aggravating factor of migraine. *Neurological Sciences.* 33; 77-80.

21. Frederick, G. & Freitag, D.O. (2007) The Cycle of Migraine: Patients' Quality of Life During and Between Migraine Attacks. *Clinical Therapeutics.* 29(5), 939-949.

22. Friedman, D. & De Ver Dye, T. (2009) Migraine and the environment. *Headache.* 49(6), 941-52.

23. Gaul, C., Totzeck, A., Kraus, U., & Straube, A. (2012). Headache and exercise. *Aktuelle Neurologie.* 39(5), 254-260.

24. Gerber, J.M. (1997) Nutrition and migraine: Review and recommended strategy. *Journal of the Neuromuscularskeletal System.* 3, 87-94.

25. Gibbs, T.S., Fleischer, A.B. Jr., Feldman, S.R., Sam, M.C., & O'Donovan, C.A. (2003). Health care utilization in patients with migraine: demographics and patterns of care in the amulatory setting. *Headache.* Apr 43(4), 330-5.

26. Gilmore, B. & Michael, M. (2011). Treatment of Acute Migraine Headache. American Family Physician. Feb 1: 83 (3): 271-80.

27. Gleitman, H. (1991) Psychology. 3rd Edition. Norton. New York.

28. Graham, B. (2006) Intelligent Investor. Harper. New York.

29. Gruber, H.J., Bernecker, C., Pailer, S., Fauler, G., Horejsi, R., Moller, R.,et al. (2010). Hyperinsulinaemia in migraineurs is associated with nitric oxide. *Cephalagia.* 30(5), 593-598.

30. Hammond, D. C. (2007). Review of the efficacy of clinical hypnosis with headaches and migraines. *International Journal of Clinical and Experimental Hypnosis, 55*(2), 207-219.

31. Hawkins, K., Wang, S., & Rupnow, M.F. (2007). Indirect cost burden of migraine in the United States. Journal of Occupational Environmental Medicine. 49, 368-74.

32. Hazard, E., Munakta, J., Bigal, M.E., Rupnow, M.F., & Lipton, R.B. (2009). The burden of migraine in the United States: Current and emerging perspectives on disease management and economic analysis. *Value in Health.* 12(1), 55-64.

33. Hofbauer, R.K., Rainville, P., Duncan, G.H. & Bushnell, M.C. (2001) Cortical representation of the sensory dimension of pain. *Journal of Neurophysiology.* July 86(1), 402-411

34. Hsu, L.K.G., Kalucy, R.S., Crisp, A.H., Koval, J., Chen, C.N., Carruthers, M., & Zilkha, K.J. (1977). Early morning migraine: Nocturnal plasma levels of catecholamines, tryptophan, glucose, and free fatty acids and sleep encephalographs. *The Lancet.* 309(8009), 447-451.

35. Jensen, M. P., & Patterson, D. R. (2006). Hypnotic Treatment of Chronic Pain. *Journal of Behavioural Medicine* 29(1), 95-124.

36. Kelley, N.E. & Tepper, D.E. (2012) Rescue therapy for acute migraine, Part 1: triptans, dihydroergotamine and magnesium. *Headache.* 52(1), 114-128.

37. Kelman, L. & Rains, J.C. (2005). Headache and sleep: examination of sleep patterns and complaints in a large clinical sample of migraineurs. *Headache: The Journal of Head & Face Pain.* Jul/Aug 45(7), 904-910.

38. Laska, E. & Sunshine, A. (1973). Anticipation of analgesia: a placebo effect. *Headache.* 13, 1-11.

39. Latsko, M., Silberstein, S., & Rosen, N. (2011). Frovatriptan as pre-emptive treatment for fasting-induced migraine. *Headache.* 51, 369-374.

40. Li, J., Shen, X., Meng, X., Zhang, Y., Lai, X. (2011). Analgesic effect and mechanism of the three TCM-herbal drug-combination Tou Feng Yu Pill on treatment of migraine. *Phytomedicine.* 18, 788-79.

41. Lipton, R.B., Stewart, W.F. Celentano, D.D. & Reed. M.L. (1992). Undiagnosed migraine headaches. A comparison of symptom-based and reported physician diagnosis. *Archives of Internal Medicine.* Jun. 152(6), 1273-8.

42. Lipton, R.B., Stewart, W.F., Diamond, S., Diamond, M.L., Reed. M. (2001). Prevalence and burden of migraine in the United States. Data from the American Migraine Study II. *Headache.* 41, 646-657.

43. Lipton, R.B. & Bigal M.E. (2005). The epidemiology of migraine. *The American Journal of Medicine.* 118(1), 3s-10s.

44. Littlewood, J.T., Glover, V., Davies, P.T.G, Gibb, C. Sandler, M., Clifford Rose, F. Red Wine as a cause of migraine. (1988). *The Lancet.* 331(8585), 558-559.

45. Lovallo, W.R. (2005). Cardiovascular reactivity: Mechanisms and pathways to cardiovascular disease. *International Journal of Psychophysiology.* 58 119-132

46. Mauskop A. & Altura, B.M. (1998). Magnesium for migraine. *CNS Drugs.* 9(3), 185-190.

47. Malenka R., & Bear M (2004). "LTP and LTD": an embarrassment of riches". *Neuron.* 44 (1), 5–21

48. Merikanges, K.R. (2012) Update on the genetics of migraine. *Headache*. Mar, 52(3), 521-2.
49. Millichap J.G. & Yee, M.M. (2003). The diet factor in paediatric and adolescent migraine. *Pediatric Neurology*. 28(1), 9-15.
50. Nusbaum, F., Redouté, J., Le Bars, D., Volckmann, P., Simon, F., Hannoun, S., et al. (2011). Chronic low-back pain modulation is enhanced by hypnotic analgesic suggestion by recruiting an emotional network: A PET imaging study. *International Journal of Clinical and Experimental Hypnosis, 59*(1), 27-44.
51. Pakalnis, A., Splaingard, M., Splaingard, D., Kring, D. & Colvin, A. (2009). Serotonin effects on Sleep and Emotional Disorders in Adolescent Migraine. *Headache: The Journal of Head & Face Pain*. 49(10), 1486-1492.
52. Posner M.I. (ed). (2004). Cognitive Neuroscience of Attention. New York: Guilford
53. Rasmussen, B.K. Migraine and tension-type headache in a general population: precipitating factors, female hormones, sleep pattern and relation to lifestyle. *Pain*. April, 53(1), 65-72.
54. Rozen, T.D. (2004). Migraine prodrome: a nose on the face. *The Lancet*. Feb, 14 (363).
55. Sándor P.S., Afra, J., Ambrosini, A., & Schoenen, J. (2000). Prophylactic treatment of migraine with beta-blockers and riboflavin: differential effects on the intensity dependence of auditory evoked cortical potentials. *Headache*. Jan, 40(1), 30-5.
56. Savona, N. (2012) quoted on website: http://www.patrickholford.com/index.php/advice/lifestagearticle/135/
57. Schoenen, J., Jacquy, J., & Lenaerts, M. (1998). Effectiveness of high-dose riboflavin in migraine prophylaxis: a randomized controlled trial. *Neurology*. 50, 466-470.
58. Schur, E.A., Noonan, C., Buchwald, D., Goldberg, & J. Afari, N. (2009). A twin study of depression and migraine: Evidence for a shared genetic vulnerability. *Headache*. 49:1:1493-1502.
59. Silberstein S. (2004). Migraine. *The Lancet*. 363(9418), 1399.
60. Silberstein, S.D., Holland, S., Freitag, F., Dodick, D.W., Argoff, C., Ashman, E. (2012). Evidence-based guideline update: Pharmacologic treatment for episodic migraine prevention in adults. *Neurology*. 78, 1337-1345.

61. Siniatchkin, M., Averkina, N., Andrasik, F., Stephani, U., Gerber, W.D. (2006). Neurophysiological reactivity before a migraine attack. *Neuroscience Letters*. 400(1-2), 121-124.

62. Society, I.H. (2012) Website: http://www.ihs-headache.org/

63. Spiegel, D. & Albert, L.H. (1983). Naloxone fails to reverse hypnotic alleviation of chronic pain. *Psychopharmacology*. 81(2), 140-143.

64. Stojanovich L. (2006). Stress as a trigger of autoimmune disease. Abstracts book: 5th International Congress on Autoimmunity, Sorrento, Italy. *Autoimmunity Reviews*. Pp 355. as cited in Stojanovich, L., Marisavljevich, D., (2008). Stress as a trigger of autoimmune disease. *Autoimmunity Reviews*. 7, 209–213

65. Stovner, L.J., Hagen, K., Jensen, R., Katsarava, Z., Lipton, R., Scher, A.I., Steiner, T.J., Zwart, J.A. (2007) The global burden of headache: a documentation of headache prevalence and disability worldwide. *Cephalagia*. 27, 193-210.

66. Tepper, S.J. (2008). A pivotal moment in 50 years of headache history: the first American migraine Study. *Headache*. May, 48(5), 730-1.

67. Tozer, B.S., Boatwright, E.A., David, P.S., Verma, D.P., Blair, J.E., Mayer, A.P. & Files, J.A. (2006). Prevention of migraine in women throughout the life span. *Mayo Clinic Proceedings. Mayo Clinic*. 81(8), 1086-1092.

68. Vargas, B.B. & Dodick, D.W. (2009). The face of Chronic Migraine: Epidemiology, Demographics, and Treamtment Strategies. *Neurological Clinics*. May, 27(2), 467-79.

69. Varkey, E., Cider, A., Carlsson, J., & Linde, M. (2008). A study to evaluate the feasibility of an aerobic exercise program in patients with migraine. *Headache*. 49, 563-570.

70. Vassalli, A. & Dijk, D.J. (2009). Review. Sleep Function: current questions and new approaches. *European Journal of Neuroscience*. 29, 1830-1841.

71. Yadav, R.K., Kalita, J. & Misra, U.K. (2010). A study of triggers of Migraine in India. *Pain Medicine*. 11, 44-47.

72. Zhuo, M., (2009). Presynaptic and Postsynaptic Mechanisms of Chronic Pain. *Molecular Neurobiology*. 40, 253-259.

Glossary

Aetiology: the origin of.

Barbiturates drugs which can have a sedative effective which ranges from mild to anaesthesia.

Beta Blockers (β-blockers) can block the effect of adrenaline and nor-adrenaline, thereby decreasing the effects of stress hormones. We do not fully understand how beta blockers work for migraine but one betablocker which is often prescribed for migraine is Propanolol.

Cheiro-oral syndrome a sensory disturbance affecting the hand and mouth unilaterally. Migraine patients might experience it as a pins and needles sensation.

Chronic migraine when a migraine patient suffers with migraine for 15 or more days each month for six months or more.

Cortical Spreading Depression (CSD): High levels of electrophysiological activity followed by a wave of inhibition. CSD is unlikely to occur in migraines without aura.

Dopamine a neurotransmitter and hormone involved in behaviour, thinking (cognition) reward, sleep, attention and other processes.

Episodic migraine when a patient suffers with migraine anywhere between no migraine days and fourteen migraine days per month.

ICHD-II International Classification of Headache Disorders II. Provides guidelines for the diagnosis and management of headache disorders.

IHS – International Headache Society. They provide criteria for diagnosing migraine. (1.1 to 1.6 diagnostic codes).

Migraineurs individuals who have been diagnosed with migraines.

Opiates: powerful painkillers derived from opium which is extracted from the Poppy plant. Codeine is an example of an opiate as is heroin.

Photophobia high sensitivity to light.

Phonophobia high sensitivity to sound.

Serotonin a neurotransmitter and hormone that is important in regulation of sleep, mood and constriction of blood vessels.

Transformed Migraine: is now sometimes called chronic migraine where attacks occur daily or almost daily. The term chronic migraine is now used interchangeably with transformed migraine. The IHS categorise chronic migraine as occurring when attacks occur on 15 or more days per month. They will generally start off as episodic migraines and progress. The severity ranges from mild to moderate.

Made in the USA
Charleston, SC
09 January 2013